JOHN 1-3

John 1-3

ANGELA LEE

CONTENTS

The Plan for This Study

This study is based on the Observation, Interpretation, Application method of Bible study. The questions and commentary are designed to help you move through these steps. Here is a brief description of the method:

Observation: What does the text say?

Read the entire text for comprehension.
Read again and consider: Who was the original audience?
What challenges or issues was the original audience facing?
What is happening in the passage?
When and where did this take place?
Why did the author write this?
Mark any keywords, repeated phrases or ideas.
Notice transition words such as "therefore", "then", "for", "so", "after" and "but".
Notice any lists, contrasts, comparisons, or types of imagery.

Interpretation: What does the text mean?

Consult different translations and trustworthy commentaries.
Look up cross-references.
What might the original hearers have thought when they received this letter?

How does this passage fit into the greater story of the Bible? (Creation-Fall-Redemption-New Creation)
Paraphrase: Rewrite the text in your own words.

Application: How do I apply it to my life?

What does this passage tell us about God?
Is there a command to obey? A promise to claim?
What does this passage tell you about your sin and your need for a Savior?
How might these truths encourage us to love the Church and love our neighbors?
How might this truth transform my life and perspective today?

~ 1 ~

INTRODUCTION TO JOHN 1-3

Observation & Interpretation

1. The gospel of John was written by John, and most evidence points to John of Zebedee, the disciple of Jesus. Read the following passages and record your observations about John and what John witnessed.

Matthew 4:18–22

[18] While walking by the Sea of Galilee, he saw two brothers, Simon (who is called Peter) and Andrew his brother, casting a net into the sea, for they were fishermen. [19] And he said to them, "Follow me, and I will make you fishers of men." [20] Immediately they left their nets and followed him. [21] And going on from there he saw two other brothers, James the son of Zebedee and John his brother, in the boat with Zebedee their father, mending their nets, and he called them. [22] Immediately they left the boat and their father and followed him.

Matthew 17:1–8

17 And after six days Jesus took with him Peter and James, and John his brother, and led them up a high mountain by themselves. [2] And he was transfigured before them, and his face shone like the sun, and his clothes became white as light. [3] And behold, there appeared to them Moses and Elijah, talking with him. [4] And Peter said to Jesus, "Lord, it is good that we are here. If you wish, I will make three tents here, one for you and one for Moses and one for Elijah." [5] He was still speaking when, behold, a bright cloud overshadowed them, and a voice from the cloud said, "This is my beloved Son,[a] with whom I am well pleased; listen to him." [6] When the disciples heard this, they fell on their faces and were terrified. [7] But Jesus came and touched them, saying, "Rise, and have no fear." [8] And when they lifted up their eyes, they saw no one but Jesus only.

Mark 5:35-43

[35] While he was still speaking, there came from the ruler's house some who said, "Your daughter is dead. Why trouble the Teacher any further?" [36] But overhearing[a] what they said, Jesus said to the ruler of the synagogue, "Do not fear, only believe." [37] And he allowed no one to follow him except Peter and James and John the brother of James. [38] They came to the house of the ruler of the synagogue, and Jesus saw a commotion, people weeping and wailing loudly. [39] And when he had entered, he said to them, "Why are you making a commotion and weeping? The child is not dead but sleeping." [40] And they laughed at him. But he put them all outside and took the child's father and mother and those who were with him and went in where the child was. [41] Taking her by the hand he said to her, "Talitha cumi," which means, "Little girl, I say to you, arise." [42] And immediately the girl got up and began walking (for she was twelve years of age), and they were immediately

overcome with amazement. [43] And he strictly charged them that no one should know this, and told them to give her something to eat.

Matthew 26:36-46 (here John is referred to as one of the sons of Zebedee.)

[36] Then Jesus went with them to a place called Gethsemane, and he said to his disciples, "Sit here, while I go over there and pray." [37] And taking with him Peter and the two sons of Zebedee, he began to be sorrowful and troubled. [38] Then he said to them, "My soul is very sorrowful, even to death; remain here, and watch[a] with me."[39] And going a little farther he fell on his face and prayed, saying, "My Father, if it be possible, let this cup pass from me; nevertheless, not as I will, but as you will." [40] And he came to the disciples and found them sleeping. And he said to Peter, "So, could you not watch with me one hour? [41] Watch and pray that you may not enter into temptation. The spirit indeed is willing, but the flesh is weak." [42] Again, for the second time, he went away and prayed, "My Father, if this cannot pass unless I drink it, your will be done." [43] And again he came and found them sleeping, for their eyes were heavy. [44] So, leaving them again, he went away and prayed for the third time, saying the same words again. [45] Then he came to the disciples and said to them, "Sleep and take your rest later on.[b] See, the hour is at hand, and the Son of Man is betrayed into the hands of sinners. [46] Rise, let us be going; see, my betrayer is at hand."

John 19:25-27 (John often referred to himself as "the disciple whom Jesus loved.")

[25] but standing by the cross of Jesus were his mother and his mother's sister, Mary the wife of Clopas, and Mary Magdalene. [26] When Jesus saw his mother and the disciple whom he loved

standing nearby, he said to his mother, "Woman, behold, your son!" [27] Then he said to the disciple, "Behold, your mother!" And from that hour the disciple took her to his own home.

John 21:20-25

[20] Peter turned and saw the disciple whom Jesus loved following them, the one who also had leaned back against him during the supper and had said, "Lord, who is it that is going to betray you?" [21] When Peter saw him, he said to Jesus, "Lord, what about this man?" [22] Jesus said to him, "If it is my will that he remain until I come, what is that to you? You follow me!" [23] So the saying spread abroad among the brothers that this disciple was not to die; yet Jesus did not say to him that he was not to die, but, "If it is my will that he remain until I come, what is that to you?"

[24] This is the disciple who is bearing witness about these things, and who has written these things, and we know that his testimony is true.

[25] Now there are also many other things that Jesus did. Were every one of them to be written, I suppose that the world itself could not contain the books that would be written.

According to your observations from question 1, describe John's relationship to Jesus.

Why do you think John's perspective of Jesus is important for us to learn from?

2. Read **John 20:30-31**. This passage is thought to give us John's purpose in writing this gospel. <u>Underline</u> what you learn about John's purpose for writing.

[30] Now Jesus did many other signs in the presence of the disciples, which are not written in this book; [31] but these are written so that you may believe that Jesus is the Christ, the Son of God, and that by believing you may have life in his name.

Commentary

How does the book of John fit within the story of the Bible?

In the beginning, God, the Son, and the Spirit dwelt together in perfect and intimate unity. God created the world by his Word as the perfect blessing for people and designed humanity to be in an intimate relationship with him. He promised Adam and Eve, the first humans, the blessing of his presence if they obeyed his words, but they listened to the serpent and disobeyed God, which separated humanity from God (Genesis 3). In Genesis 3:15, God promised to rescue his people through a seed of the woman and dwell with them again. God continued engaging with the broken world and inviting people into relationship, and he related to humanity through covenants. With Abraham, he made a covenant to make his family a nation, provide a place for them, and to bless them with a blessing that would bless every family on earth (Genesis 12,15). Abraham's family became the nation of Israel. Through many trials and wanderings, including enslavement in Egypt (Exodus 1), God was faithful to keep his covenant and rescue His people. He used Moses to deliver Israel from Egypt, and this deliverance became a marker to help them remember God's salvation and point them to a greater deliverance to come.

Building on the covenant he had made with Abraham, God made the Mosaic covenant with Israel, promising them a relationship with him as a nation of priests, and God gave them his law at Mount Sinai to show them how to live faithfully to him. He promised that if Israel obeyed his law, they would be his "treasured possession". God loved his people, and they were to love him in return. He revealed himself to Moses as the God of "steadfast love and faithfulness" (Exodus 34). But the Israelites' sinful state made it so they couldn't dwell with God or hear his words without mediators. So, through Moses, the sacrificial system was put in place, and the tabernacle was built where God dwelt amongst His people. The priests were called to teach Israel God's commands and intercede for the people's sin through sacrifices (Deuteronomy 27-28, Exodus 19-31).

Israel claimed their promised land in the book of Joshua, but they still struggled to be faithful to God's covenant by fully taking the land. Later, God appointed judges to guide them, and at the request of Israel, kings ruled over them (I Samuel 8). During the reign of the second king, God made another covenant with King David promising that one of David's descendants would remain on the throne forever. The judges and kings of Israel were to keep God's law, but instead, they often led the people astray. So, God continued to raise up prophets who were to speak to his people on his behalf.

Later in Israel's history, King David dreamed of a temple; it would be a house where God's tabernacle might dwell, God's word would be spoken, and others would come to worship Him. God used David's son Solomon to build this temple, and a second was built about 500 years later under the leadership of Ezra.

Israel knew of God's covenant promises to be their God and their covenant obligation to love the Lord their God and obey His law out of loyalty to him (Exodus 20, Deuteronomy 27-28). They knew God had promised to send a forever King in David's line (2 Samuel 7), and God promised to restore them if they repented of their sin (Deuteronomy 30:1-10). Even with all this knowledge and all this hope, God's people went their own way, chose their own gods, and refused to repent. The Kingdom soon divided into two kingdoms at the end of Solomon's reign: Israel and Judah. They continued to wander and live unfaithfully under wayward kings and priests, and they ignored the prophets that God sent to confront them.

God's people endured exile under the nation of Babylon. And in 538 B.C., some of Israel would be gathered with the nation of Judah under King Cyrus's decree to go back to the house of the Lord. But the Jewish people continued to be tossed about under the heavy hand of powerful nations for 400 more years. In 63 B.C., they began to live under the occupation of the Roman Empire. This is when John's testimony begins.

John opens his gospel and announces that Jesus came as the true Prophet, the Word of God made flesh (John 1:14), the true King, a descendent of David, the better deliverer Moses (John 1:17), and a merciful high priest. He would be the lamb of God, the final sacrifice who takes away the sin of the world (John 1:29). Jesus came to his own people, Israel, to dwell and "tabernacle" among them as the new temple and the long-awaited rescuer (John 1:14, 2:18-22). John's testimony says that Jesus is the "grace and truth", the "steadfast love and faithfulness" that Moses saw — the presence of the Father (John 1:16). He is the Messiah the Old Testament pointed to, and to all who believe in his name, he has given them the right to become children of God (John 1:12). John proclaims that through Christ, God invites humanity back into the intimacy with Him we were created for.

Who wrote the Gospel of John?

The Gospel of John was written by John. And while there is one more 'John' viewed as a possibility, most evidence points to the writer being John of Zebedee. John usually refers to himself as "the disciple Jesus loved" in his narrative, and the "beloved disciple" claims to have written the book in John 21:20-24 saying, "This is the disciple who is bearing witness about these things, and who has written these things, and we know that his testimony is true."

John was with Jesus from the very beginning of his ministry (1:35-40), at the last supper (13:23), at the cross (19:26-27), at the empty tomb (20:2), and he is mentioned after the resurrection (21:20). He was one of Jesus's disciples in his close circle, and he is often found in the company of Peter. Along with this internal evidence of John's authorship, there are also many statements by church fathers like Irenaeus who tell us that John wrote John.

When and where was the Gospel of John written?

Tradition tells us that John was most likely written in the 80s or 90s in Ephesus, and it was the latest of the four gospels. Church fathers like Irenaeus and Clement made statements confirming this as well. John uses a mature and developed language to describe the divinity of Christ that was likely a result of a later and developed Christology. He seems to leave out significant material from Matthew, Mark, and Luke and adds his own unique perspective. This shows us that John likely felt no need to repeat what had already been written. John also goes to great lengths to present Jesus as the fulfillment of the temple, so many assume he was writing after the destruction of the temple in 70 A.D to assure Jewish believers the temple was no longer needed.

Structure and Outline of John

John 1:1–18 — Prologue: An Introduction to the Book.

John 1:19 - 11:57 — Book of Signs: Signs of Jesus's Messianic identity and corresponding teaching.

John 12–20 — Book of Passion: The last week of Jesus's life leading to His death.

John 21 — Epilogue.

Structure and Outline of John 1-3

In this study, we will focus on the first three chapters of John.

John 1:1–18 — Prologue: An Introduction to the Book.

John 1:19–51 — Prelude to Jesus's public ministry.

- John the Baptist's relationship to Jesus and his witness about Jesus (John 1:19-34).
- Jesus gains His first disciples (John 1:35-51).

John 2-3 —Jesus's early ministry

- The first sign: Water to wine (John 2:1-11).

- Jesus clears and replaces the temple (John 2:12–25).

- Jesus and Nicodemus and follow-up teaching (John 3:1-21).

- John the Baptist continuing witness and follow-up teaching (John 3:22-36).[1]

What is the purpose of John 1-3, and what themes did John use to bring out this purpose?

The purpose of John's gospel is stated in John 20:30–31:

"Now Jesus did many other signs in the presence of the disciples, which are not written in this book; but these are written so that you may believe that Jesus is the Christ, the Son of God, and that by believing you may have life in his name."

John wrote his gospel, likely primarily to a Jewish audience, to convince them that Jesus is the "Christ" or "Anointed" Messiah they had been waiting for. First century Jews expected the Messiah to come as the eternal King, the Son of David who would reign forever. He would be the fulfillment of Israel's prophecies, priesthood, kingly line, and all its history. John shows us that **Jesus is the fulfillment of the Old Testament**, and, therefore, he is the promised Christ. Throughout this study, we will carefully search the John 1-3 for Old Testament references and allusions to help us have a deeper biblical theological perspective of his testimony. This facet of the gospel of John will strengthen our faith as we explore the fact that our Christian faith is not just in a first century man, but in one who has been promised since the beginning of time.

Closely related to Jesus's fulfillment of the Old Testament is the theme of **Jesus's Divinity.** While all the gospels present us with a Divine Jesus, John uses the most explicit language to describe his power, glory, and his role as heavenly King.[2] He uses vertical dualism like light vs. darkness and life vs. death that lifts the reader's gaze to contrast the heavenly with the earthly. Church father Clement of Alexandria was recorded as saying, "John, perceiving that the external facts had been made plain [in the other canonical gospels], composed a spiritual gospel." In early Christian art, the four gospels were often depicted as the four creatures seen in Ezekiel 1 and Revelation (the lion, the bull, the angel, and the eagle). John was depicted as the eagle, soaring into the heavens. His gospel has always been viewed as having a high and holy view of Christ and one that explores the divine nature of Jesus. John opens his gospel with a burst of worship that will lead us to marvel at the beauty and divinity of Jesus Christ.

Lastly, John leads us in how to respond to Jesus through the **example of John the Baptist.** John the Baptist not only spoke helpful and informative words about Jesus, but his whole life was lived in humble service to Christ. He boldly and proudly proclaimed, "I am not the Christ." And his ministry was to be "a voice" calling out to others to point people to the true Christ. As we behold the Jesus of the gospel of John, our response should be to imitate John the Baptist, to receive Christ, and "have life in His name" (John 20:31). In this study, we will consider John's faithful ministry and humble heart as he lived for the glory of Jesus as a child of God.

Application & Reflection

1. How does John's relationship with Jesus inform the way we read his gospel?

2. What do you want to learn from this study about Jesus fulfilling the Old Testament, His Divinity, and John the Baptist's witness to him?

3. What questions or thoughts do you have about the gospel of John?

~ 2 ~

JOHN 1:1-5

Observation & Interpretation

Read John 1:1-5 and consider the following questions.

1 In the beginning was the Word, and the Word was with God, and the Word was God. ²He was in the beginning with God. ³All things were made through him, and without him was not any thing made that was made. ⁴In him was life, and the life was the light of men. ⁵The light shines in the darkness, and the darkness has not overcome it.

1. Underline and/or record any repeated words that you see in John 1:1-5.

2. John 1:14 will reveal that when John says, "the Word," he is talking about Jesus. According to John 1:1-2, what are some characteristics of the relationship between Jesus and God?

3. The phrase "In the beginning" is a reference to **Genesis 1:1**, the very first verse in the Bible:

1 In the beginning, God created the heavens and the earth.

What do you think John's intention is in associating Jesus with Genesis 1?

4. According to John 1:3, what is the relationship between Jesus and Creation, or "things that were made"?

5. While John's language was likely partly informed by Greek philosophy and the word "logos", (see commentary), we can be even more certain that his use of "word" was informed by what the "word" does in the Old Testament. Read the following verses where God's "Word" is described and consider: what is the role of "the Word"?

Genesis 1:3, 9

[3] And God said, "Let there be light," and there was light.

[9] And God said, "Let the waters under the heavens be gathered together into one place, and let the dry land appear." And it was so.

Deuteronomy 32:45–47

[45] And when Moses had finished speaking all these words to all Israel, [46] he said to them, "Take to heart all the words by which I am warning you today, that you may command them to your children, that they may be careful to do all the words of this law. [47] For it is no empty word for you, but your very life, and by this word you shall live long in the land that you are going over the Jordan to possess."

Psalm 33:6

[6] By the word of the Lord the heavens were made,
   and by the breath of his mouth all their host.

Psalm 107:20

[20] He sent out his word and healed them,
   and delivered them from their destruction.

Psalm 119:105

[105] Your word is a lamp to my feet
   and a light to my path.

Isaiah 55:10-11

[10] "For as the rain and the snow come down from heaven
   and do not return there but water the earth,
making it bring forth and sprout,
   giving seed to the sower and bread to the eater,
[11] so shall my word be that goes out from my mouth;
   it shall not return to me empty,
but it shall accomplish that which I purpose,
   and shall succeed in the thing for which I sent it.

6. How does the insight from question 5 help you understand what John is saying about Jesus?

7. What characteristics of Jesus do you see in John 1:1-5?

8. John 1:5 is the first of many times John will refer to Jesus as the "light." John uses this word poetically and is intentionally ambiguous here; "light" likely has multiple meanings. Considering what you have seen in this passage about creation and the word, what do you think John means by "light" in verse 5?

Commentary

As John opens his testimony of Jesus, the prologue reveals his antiquity and his nature. The prologue in John 1:1-18 serves as an introduction to the person and work of Jesus that will be expanded upon in the rest of the gospel.

John 1:1

John uses the phrase "In the beginning", reminding the audience of the Creator from Genesis 1 who has been, who has always known them, and who has always revealed himself to them. John's use of "the Word" has led to much debate and study, and John is probably using this phrase for more than one meaning. (John enjoys using words for their multiple meanings and he does this many times throughout the book). He says in the beginning was the Word, and the Greek for this is "logos". The Greeks' worldview taught that there was an eternal and ancient principle of "logos" that undergirded everything. The term Logos referred to the structure and order of the universe. Josh Moody eloquently states that "John makes the case that the logos- the immaterial intelligence which alone can explain rational thought, the laws of science, and the mathematical structure of reality — is actually a Person to whom he witnesses."[3]

However, we know that John was Jewish, and that in the rest of his testimony of Jesus, he repeatedly refers to the Old Testament. So, while it is likely that John was referring to the word "logos" to appeal to his Greek audience, we can be even more certain that when John refers to Jesus as the "Word", he is thinking of the many purposes and definitions of the "word" in the Old Testament. In the OT, God's "word" relates to God's creation (Psalm 33:6), revelation (Psalm 19), deliverance (Isaiah 55:11), life (Deuteronomy 32:47), healing (Psalm 107:20), and wisdom (Proverbs 8:22).[4] The unfolding of His word brings light and life (Psalm 119:130). John is saying that this life-giving, sustaining, and powerful Word has been made flesh in Jesus Christ (John 1:14).

John traces the testimony of Jesus's ministry back to creation. This Word was from the beginning, He was with God, and He was God. John goes to great lengths to explain that Jesus was not new in the first century, but He is the beginning, and He is God.

John 1:2–3

What is his relationship to God? He is with the Creator; all things were made through him and without him nothing was made. The Word is distinct from God, but he is completely unified with God, and they belong together.[5] Jesus was not created but he is one with the Creator. John states this positively and negatively. Jesus's role in creation is often referred to in the New Testament, and here it seems John is saying that the Father created, and He did it through Christ, "the Word".

John 1:4–5

"In Him was life, and the life was the light of men." When he came, he brought life that illuminated the life in the men that he created. Just as God spoke into the dark void and brought order and light (Genesis 1:3-5), God through Christ came as the Word made flesh to speak light and life to the dark void of sin and death. Morris explains, "John is preparing the way for the thought which he will develop throughout his Gospel, that Jesus is *the* life-bringer and light-bearer."[6] He shone in the darkness and emptiness of what men's life had become apart from Him. The Light had come, and the dark void did not overcome it.

Application and Reflection

1. What characteristic of Jesus stands out to you from John 1:1-5?

2. John presents Jesus as the "Word of God" made flesh. What benefit of God's word stands out to you from this lesson?

What benefit of God's word do you desire to understand and/or experience more of this week?

How might this desire lead you to pray?

3. In these verses, John is telling us that the Christian faith is not in a first-century man but in the One who has been from the very beginning. How does this encourage, comfort, or challenge you?

~ 3 ~

JOHN 1:6-13

Observation and Interpretation

Read John 1:6-13 and consider the following questions.

⁶ There was a man sent from God, whose name was John. ⁷ He came as a witness, to bear witness about the light, that all might believe through him. ⁸ He was not the light, but came to bear witness about the light.

⁹ The true light, which gives light to everyone, was coming into the world.

¹⁰ He was in the world, and the world was made through him, yet the world did not know him. ¹¹ He came to his own, and his own people did not receive him. ¹² But to all who did receive him, who believed in his name, he gave the right to become children of God, ¹³ who were born, not of blood nor of the will of the flesh nor of the will of man, but of God.

1. Underline and/or take note of repeated words and phrases in John 1:6-9.

What do you think this repetition aims to convey about John the Baptist?

2. The Old Testament prophets told of a "forerunner" to prepare the way for Jesus, and this forerunner came in John the Baptist. Read the following verses and underline the statements about John's purpose. (John is mentioned in Malachi 3:1 and Isaiah 40:3).

Malachi 3:1-3

3 "Behold, I send my messenger, and he will prepare the way before me. And the Lord whom you seek will suddenly come to his temple; and the messenger of the covenant in whom you delight, behold, he is coming, says the Lord of hosts. ² But who can endure the day of his coming, and who can stand when he appears? For he is like a refiner's fire and like fullers' soap. ³ He will sit as a refiner and purifier of silver, and he will purify the sons of Levi and refine them like gold and silver, and they will bring offerings in righteousness to the Lord.

Isaiah 40:1-5, 9

40 Comfort, comfort my people, says your God.
² Speak tenderly to Jerusalem,
    and cry to her
that her warfare is ended,

that her iniquity is pardoned,
that she has received from the Lord's hand
    double for all her sins.

³ A voice cries:
"In the wilderness prepare the way of the Lord;
    make straight in the desert a highway for our God.
⁴ Every valley shall be lifted up,
    and every mountain and hill be made low;
the uneven ground shall become level,
    and the rough places a plain.
⁵ And the glory of the Lord shall be revealed,
    and all flesh shall see it together,
    for the mouth of the Lord has spoken."

⁹ Go on up to a high mountain,
    O Zion, herald of good news;
lift up your voice with strength,
    O Jerusalem, herald of good news;
    lift it up, fear not;
say to the cities of Judah,
    "Behold your God!"

Summarize John the Baptist's role in preparing the way for Christ:

3. Verses 1-5 introduced Christ as the Word "in the beginning", and in verses 6-9 John shows us Jesus had a forerunner prophesied in the Old Testament. What do you think John aims to communicate with these two points?

4. In verses 10-11, John begins to explain the relationship between the "Word" and the world. What is the relationship between:

The Word and the world—

The Word and His "own people"—

5. The world and God's own people "did not receive him", but what does God grant according to verses 12-13?

To whom does God grant this to?

Commentary

After John shared that Jesus was God's Word made flesh, he wrote about "the witness" to this Word. Malachi and Isaiah prophesied one would come to "prepare the way" as a forerunner for the Messiah. John the author, (and the other three gospel writers), include John the Baptist in their introductions. In doing so, they point out that Jesus was the Messiah predicted and foretold from the beginning.

John 1:6–8

Jesus had a witness sent from God whose name was John. John the Baptist's origin story is wonderful and miraculous in its own way, but the author doesn't focus on that here. In these verses, John the author references John the Baptist to tell us he came as a witness to share about who Jesus was – the light of the world. John the Baptist's role was to be a witness so that through his testimony, all might believe in Christ. John himself was a man; he himself was not the light, but he came to bear witness about the light.

John 1:9–11

The true light was Jesus, who enlightens and offers the light. This light was coming into the world, but when he came, the world did not recognize him or accept him. He came to his own people, the Jews, the people he had been faithful to for generations, but they did not receive him. Andreas Kostenberger notes, "The world rejecting God is tragic, even more tragic is the Covenant peoples' rejection of the One they were seeking".[7]

John 1:12-13

Even though his chosen people rejected him, there were some who did receive Jesus. And to all who did receive him by believing in his name, he gave them a new status. To believe in a "name" to this original audience meant to trust and embrace the whole essence and personality of a person, in this case, to believe and trust in the person of Jesus Christ. Those who believed in his name were given the right, by grace through faith, to become the children of God.

Then John expands on the miraculous nature of their new birth. The Jews prided themselves in the idea that their ancestors and heritage gave them the "right" to be God's children, but John is correcting this belief. Morris eloquently says, "Nothing human, however great or excellent, can bring about the birth in which he speaks."[8] The true children of God were of both Jewish and Gentile descent, but they were born and became God's children not by their heritage or family line, or their own efforts or choosing, but born of God and his Spirit by his grace through Jesus Christ.

Application & Reflection

1. John tells us that John the Baptist's purpose was entirely wrapped up in his witness to the glory of Christ. What does this tell you about the way God uses people in his plan of redemption?

In what ways do you think our calling as Christ-followers is like the calling and purpose of John the Baptist?

2. How have you witnessed the reality of the world's response to Jesus as described in John 1:10-11?

3. What is your response to God's gracious offer in John 1:12-13?

Take some time to thank and praise Jesus for His indescribable gift using John 1:12-13 as a prompt.

~ 4 ~

JOHN 1:14-18

Observation & Interpretation

Read John 1:14-18 and consider the following questions.

¹⁴ And the Word became flesh and dwelt among us, and we have seen his glory, glory as of the only Son from the Father, full of grace and truth. ¹⁵ (John bore witness about him, and cried out, "This was he of whom I said, 'He who comes after me ranks before me, because he was before me.'") ¹⁶ For from his fullness we have all received, grace upon grace. ¹⁷ For the law was given through Moses; grace and truth came through Jesus Christ. ¹⁸ No one has ever seen God; God the only Son, who is at the Father's side, he has made him known.

1. What words or phrases are repeated in these verses?

What do you think John aims to convey with this repetition?

2. In verse 14, John refers to the "Word" from verse 1. What does he say the word did?

What is "seen" as a result, according to 14b?

3. This passage has many references to God "dwelling" among us and being "seen." And it will help us to understand what John had in mind from the Old Testament. The word "dwelt" here (vs. 14) means "pitched his tabernacle" or "lived in his tent." Read **Exodus 33:7–11** to reflect on the times God dwelt among His people and record your observations.

[7] Now Moses used to take the tent and pitch it outside the camp, far off from the camp, and he called it the tent of meeting. And everyone who sought the Lord would go out to the tent of meeting, which was outside the camp. [8] Whenever Moses went out to the tent, all the people would rise up, and each would stand at his tent door, and watch Moses until he had gone into the tent. [9] When Moses entered the tent, the pillar of cloud would descend and stand at the entrance of the tent, and the Lord would speak with Moses. [10] And when all the people saw the pillar of cloud standing at the entrance of the tent, all the people would rise up and worship, each at his tent door. [11] Thus the Lord used to speak to Moses face to face, as a man speaks to his friend. When Moses turned again into the camp, his assistant Joshua the son of Nun, a young man, would not depart from the tent.

How does this passage in Exodus help you understand what John meant when he wrote, "the Word became flesh and *dwelt* among us?"

4. What additional insight do we gain from verse 15 about John the Baptist?

5. According to verse 16, what do we receive as the result of Jesus's coming?

6. John explains the magnitude of Jesus's "fullness" by explaining why His coming is even more glorious than God's revelation of His glory through the law. "The Law came through Moses" when he received it at Mount Sinai (Exodus 19) and it was a gracious gift of revelation of God's character and will. But "grace and truth came through Jesus Christ." Take some time to reflect: why is Jesus Christ's coming an even more gracious gift than the law of Moses?

7. The references to "glory" and "seeing God" should remind us of the times God has displayed His glory before. In Exodus 33:17–34:8, Moses asked to see God's glory, but God only showed him his back. The glory that Moses saw revealed that God is full of steadfast love and faithfulness. John 1:18 reminds us that while Moses was the closest, no one had ever seen God. What exception is presented in John 1:18?

9. With the insight of the previous questions in mind, read **John 1:18** in the different translations below. Then, paraphrase this verse in your own words.

NIV: [18] No one has ever seen God, but the one and only Son, who is himself God and is in closest relationship with the Father, has made him known.

CSB: [18] No one has ever seen God. The one and only Son, who is himself God and is at the Father's side—he has revealed him.

NASB: [18] No one has seen God at any time; God the only *Son*, who is in the arms of the Father, He has explained *Him*.

NLT: [18] No one has ever seen God. But the unique One, who is himself God, is near to the Father's heart. He has revealed God to us.

Paraphrase John 1:18 in your own words:

Commentary

In these verses we have the climax to the prologue. As readers familiar with this text, we have known that John was speaking about Jesus, but John built up to revealing this. The Word that was from the beginning, whom John the Baptist bore witness to, became flesh. Andreas Kostenberger says, "Now, at last, the veil is lifted and the Word, the light, and the only Son of the Father are finally identified as Jesus Christ."[9]

John 1:14

The Word became flesh—Jesus took on human nature and dwelt among us as God has always dwelt among His people. Scholars help us see that the Greek phrase "dwelt among us" here means "the word pitched his tabernacle" or "lived in his tent" among us. Before the temple was built, God dwelled with His people in the tabernacle and lived among them. God pursued and fellowship with His people in the tabernacle, and this passage tells us that God came to dwell and fellowship with His people in the person of Jesus Christ.

The allusion to the tabernacle helps us understand the second part of the verse: "we have seen His glory." God's glory was present in the tabernacle, and on Jesus, the incarnate Word, rests the true glory of God. D.A. Carson explains, "the ultimate manifestation of the presence of God amongst human beings is found in Jesus Christ."[10] This glory, the visible manifestation of God, was full of "grace and truth". Hebrew scholars help us understand that the "grace and truth" in verses 16-17 probably allude to "steadfast love and faithfulness" of God in the OT. This expression that occurs repeatedly to describe God's character in the OT, especially in God's revelation to Moses in Exodus 33-34. This verse is saying that

God's character, full of grace and truth, is manifested most perfectly in Jesus.

John 1:15

Jesus is the one John the Baptist bore witness about. Even though Jesus became flesh after John the Baptist was born, Jesus is superior because He has always been. In Jewish society, birth order was important. But John makes sure this is clear: even though John the Baptist was born first, Jesus was from eternity past, and He was greater.

John 1:16-17

"From His fullness we have received grace upon grace" (vs.16). This phrase "Grace upon grace" is a source of debate, but many have explained that the phrase can be translated, "grace instead of grace".[11] Or as the NIV says, "Grace in place of grace." And the 'graces' are explained by verse 17. The first "grace" given seems to be the grace that came through Moses. God's giving of the law to Moses is the backdrop for this passage. The ESV Study Bible says, "The giving of the law and the coming of Jesus Christ mark decisive events in the history of salvation. In the law, God graciously revealed His character and righteous requirements to the nation of Israel. Jesus, however, marked the final, definitive revelation of God's grace and truth."[12] The law and God's revelation of his character came through Moses – and it was indeed a source of grace, and an important mark in salvation history. God gave His law so that his people could be with him as his treasured possession. The law gave a way of life, boundary ways and prescriptions for flourishing that would allow God's created people to live in line with their created order.

The "graces" that are being compared are not the bad vs. the good but the good vs. the better. Both the law and Jesus are gracious gifts; however, one surpasses and supplants the other. The law was gracious, but Jesus is the greater Moses and offers a greater grace.

The gracious gift of the covenant law has now been fulfilled and surpassed by the "grace and truth" (John 1:17) of God manifested in Jesus Christ. Jesus offers a grace higher than the grace of the law because he fulfilled the law. We couldn't live up to the standard of the law. Jesus obeyed the law on our behalf and came as the manifestation of God's character—then, he offers us the grace to know and be with God. Because of Jesus, we are free to pursue holiness and live within his law, but we can also be showered with the grace of forgiveness when we step outside of those boundaries. He is truly the greatest gift of all.

Through the law, God's people still did not see or know Him intimately. But the glorious presence of God, the fulfillment of his law, access to intimacy with the Father, and "grace and truth" in their unveiled splendor came through Jesus Christ.

John 1:18

No one had ever seen God, but Jesus was a unique exception; He had been with God, "at the father's side" since eternity past. Language scholars help us understand that the English translations, like the ESV "at the father's side", do not quite capture the intimacy implied here. The Greek phrase offers a picture of the Son resting "in the bosom" or "in the chest" of the father like a father embracing his son as his son rests on his chest. No one had ever seen God, but Jesus has always known Him intimately.

This verse likely has a reference to Moses as well, for though Moses was highly esteemed, in the system he set up, nobody could "see" God.[13] God passed before Moses and told him of his "grace and truth" in Exodus 34:6, but he covered Moses with his hand, and Moses only saw his back. Through Christ, God incarnate came to dwell amongst his people and make the "grace and truth" of the Father known. The glory that formerly could not be seen by the Israelites was displayed in the Son coming down to them.

This method of displaying glory may sound strange to us; we tend to think of "glory" as a grand elaborate show of power and strength. But it was the incarnation, when the Word was made flesh, that led the angels to proclaim, "Glory to God in the Highest!" (Luke 2:14). God displays the truest manifestation of his "grace and truth", his glory, by Jesus's self-sacrifice, humility, and incarnation.

Application & Reflection

1. John's comparison between Jesus and Moses in John 1:16-17 helps us understand that the law is a good gift, but Jesus is the most glorious gift of all. Do you tend to view the God's law as a good thing or a hindrance/source of fear?

2. What would it look like to live in light of the fact that the law is a gift, but Jesus is the greatest and most gracious gift?

3. In John 1:14 and 18, John explains that Jesus displays his glory by coming to earth and humbling himself as the word made flesh. Jesus came to be with his people and display God's grace and truth. What is your response to God's persistence to "dwell" in the midst of his people?

Take some time to thank and praise God for his humility and self-sacrifice using John 1:14, 18 as a prompt

[14] *And the Word became flesh and dwelt among us, and we have seen his glory, glory as of the only Son from the Father, full of grace and truth....*[18] *No one has ever seen God; God the only Son, who is at the Father's side, he has made him known.*

~ 5 ~

JOHN 1:19-28

Observation & Interpretation

Read John 1:19-28 and consider the following questions.

¹⁹ And this is the testimony of John, when the Jews sent priests and Levites from Jerusalem to ask him, "Who are you?" ²⁰ He confessed, and did not deny, but confessed, "I am not the Christ." ²¹ And they asked him, "What then? Are you Elijah?" He said, "I am not." "Are you the Prophet?" And he answered, "No." ²² So they said to him, "Who are you? We need to give an answer to those who sent us. What do you say about yourself?" ²³ He said, "I am the voice of one crying out in the wilderness, 'Make straight the way of the Lord,' as the prophet Isaiah said."

²⁴ (Now they had been sent from the Pharisees.) ²⁵ They asked him, "Then why are you baptizing, if you are neither the Christ, nor Elijah, nor the Prophet?" ²⁶ John answered them, "I baptize with water, but among you stands one you do not know,²⁷ even he who comes after me, the strap of whose sandal I am not worthy to untie."²⁸ These things took place in Bethany across the Jordan, where John was baptizing.

1. This section (John 1:19-34) is the testimony of John the Baptist—the "witness" to the "Word." According to verse 19, who came to question John?

What did they ask John and what was his response according to verse 20?

2. The authorities assumed John thought he was someone significant. So, they asked John whether he is one of two prominent figures whom the Jews expected to come before Christ came. Read the prophecies below and record your observations about Elijah and the Prophet.

Elijah — Malachi 4:5-6

[5] "Behold, I will send you Elijah the prophet before the great and awesome day of the Lord comes. [6] And he will turn the hearts of fathers to their children and the hearts of children to their fathers, lest I come and strike the land with a decree of utter destruction."

The Prophet — Deuteronomy 18:15–18

[15] The Lord your God will raise up for you a prophet like me from among you, from your brothers—it is to him you shall listen— [16] just as you desired of the Lord your God at Horeb on the day of the assembly, when you said, 'Let me not hear again the voice of the Lord my God or see this great fire any more, lest I

die.' ¹⁷ And the Lord said to me, 'They are right in what they have spoken. ¹⁸ I will raise up for them a prophet like you from among their brothers. And I will put my words in his mouth, and he shall speak to them all that I command him.

3. John denied being either Elijah or the Prophet, but he answered them saying he fulfilled different Old Testament prophecy. He quoted from Isaiah and said he was "a voice crying in the wilderness"; the context of this passage is that Isaiah was telling God's people to prepare for God to bring them home from exile. Read **Isaiah 40:1-5** and record your observations.

40 Comfort, comfort my people, says your God.
² Speak tenderly to Jerusalem,
   and cry to her
that her warfare is ended,
   that her iniquity is pardoned,
that she has received from the Lord's hand
   double for all her sins.

³ A voice cries:
"In the wilderness prepare the way of the Lord;
   make straight in the desert a highway for our God.
⁴ Every valley shall be lifted up,
   and every mountain and hill be made low;
the uneven ground shall become level,
   and the rough places a plain.
⁵ And the glory of the Lord shall be revealed,
   and all flesh shall see it together,
   for the mouth of the Lord has spoken."

What do you think John was saying by quoting this prophecy?

4. John gave the authorities a solid answer, but what seemed to be the primary concern of the Jews according to John 1:24-25?

5. How did John answer in John 1:26-27 and what did he say about Jesus (the one who "comes after" him)?

Commentary

In John 1:6-8 we were introduced to John the Baptist—the "witness to the word", and here in John 1:19-28 we are given more of his testimony.

John 1:19–22

These verses describe a conversation that sparked after the Jews had sent religious authorities to question John the Baptist. D.A Carson calls these leaders the "temple police"[14] and they seemed to mostly be concerned with the fact that John was baptizing. Scholars help us understand that John's baptism was related to a kind of ritual cleansing that was common in John's day for Gentile converts. Gentiles were considered unclean, and if they wanted to convert to Judaism and be brought into the covenant community of Israel, they needed to repent of their sins and submit to this ritual cleansing. But what John was doing was unheard of in his day because he was administering this baptism to the Jews. (And it was insulting to the religious leaders that John claimed the children of Abraham needed to go through cleansing.) By performing this baptism, John was demonstrating that even for the children of Abraham, repentance and faith were necessary for entrance into the Kingdom.[15] Another difference of John's baptism was that in the proselyte baptism, it was typical for the convert to baptize himself, but John was baptizing these people, even though he had no official or priestly authority to do so (Sproul).[16] These religious leaders were concerned; they asked, "Who are you?" And John responded by confessing freely that he was not the Christ. John the Baptist never claimed to be the Christ, but since he was baptizing, these religious leaders could see that he seemed to be (or thought of himself as) someone significant. So, they asked, "Who are you then, are you Elijah?" Elijah had been prophesied to return before the end times. But John said he was not Elijah. (Later in Jesus's ministry, Jesus seemed to contradict this and informed the disciples that John was "Elijah who was to come" (Matthew 11:14); but we can assume Jesus understood John's role better that John did.) The Pharisees kept searching their scriptures and knowledge for who John could be. Next they asked, "Are you the Prophet?" In Deuteronomy 18, Moses had prophesied that a greater Prophet would come. But to this question, John said "no". So, the religious leaders kept asking questions because "they needed to give an answer to those who sent them." They finally asked, "What do you say about yourself?"

John 1:23

John gave them an answer according to the Old Testament. He quoted Isaiah 40:3 and explained that he was a "voice" crying out in the wilderness saying, "prepare the way for the Lord; make straight in the desert a highway for our God." In its context, Isaiah 40 calls for an improvement of the road system to prepare the way for God's people to return from exile. When the people of Isaiah's day heard this message, this would have given the nation of Judah hope that they would one day be free to return to Jerusalem after their suffering in exile under Babylon. But this rescue pointed to a greater rescue.

Just like God made a way for his people to come home in Isaiah's day, through Christ, God would lead a new Exodus to save his people from slavery to sin. And Isaiah 40 predicted a forerunner, a "voice" (Isaiah 40:3), and one who would prepare the way for the Savior. This is who John the Baptist knew himself to be. The Gospel Transformation Study Bible explains, "John straddled the Old and New Testaments like a bridge...he was the last of the Old Testament Prophets, and at the same time he was the first herald of the arrival of God's promised Kingdom in Jesus."[17] But the religious leaders didn't seem to understand. Many Pharisees were noble and diligently studied the scriptures, but sadly, they were often so focused on their many regulations and the outward appearance of things that they missed the substance.

John 1:24–28

The religious leaders missed John's announcement of the Messiah. Verse 24 clarifies that they were sent from Pharisees, and their aim and purpose was likely to enforce Jewish law. John tried to point them to Jesus, but they remained focused on their task. They hadn't received their answer yet, so they got straight to the point. They asked, "Then why are you baptizing, if you are neither Christ, nor Elijah, nor the Prophet?"

John answered them, "I baptize with water, but among you stands one that you do not know, even he who comes after me, the strap of whose sandal I am not worthy to untie." The NLT translates John's statement, "I'm not even worthy to be his slave..." In some ways, in Jewish tradition, a disciple functioned as a personal slave of their Rabbi. However, as R.C Sproul explains, "...one thing that differentiated a disciple in a rabbinical school from an actual bondslave was that the disciple was never required to take care of the shoes or the sandals of his teacher. A slave could be reduced to this humiliating task, but not a disciple."[18] John was telling them there was no need to look at him... his worthiness compared to Christ's worthiness rendered him even lower than a slave. John deflects the attention from himself and points the people to Jesus. John didn't want to draw attention to his own ministry, he only wanted his ministry to point to the One who was to come.

Application & Reflection

1. The priests and Levites sent by the Jews were concerned with John obeying man made rules, and so they missed his declaration of the good news of Jesus's coming. Can you think of a time when focusing on man-made rules and agendas led you to "miss" Jesus?

What did you learn about yourself from this experience?

What did you learn about Jesus?

2. How might the knowledge that our hearts are prone to prioritize our own agenda over experiencing Christ lead you to pray this week?

3. John knew his role and assignment in God's kingdom, and it seems like this helped him stay focused on his task (even while he faced distraction, hardship, and accusation from the Pharisees). Read the following verses about our role and assignment as Christ followers and consider the following questions.

Ephesians 2:4-10

[4] But God, being rich in mercy, because of the great love with which he loved us, [5] even when we were dead in our trespasses, made us alive together with Christ—by grace you have been saved—[6] and raised us up with him and seated us with him in the heavenly places in Christ Jesus, [7] so that in the coming ages he might show the immeasurable riches of his grace in kindness toward us in Christ Jesus. [8] For by grace you have been saved through faith. And this is not your own doing; it is the gift of God, [9] not a result of works, so that no one may boast. [10] For we are his workmanship, created in Christ Jesus for good works, which God prepared beforehand, that we should walk in them.

1 Peter 2:9-10

[9] But you are a chosen race, a royal priesthood, a holy nation, a people for his own possession, that you may proclaim the excellencies of him who called you out of darkness into his marvelous light. [10] Once you were not a people, but now you are God's people; once you had not received mercy, but now you have received mercy.

How might understanding your purpose and assignment help you to stay focused this week?

How might this lead you to pray?

4. John made every effort to move the attention from himself to Jesus. How is John the Baptist's example of selfless service and faith encouraging to you?

How is his example challenging to you?

What steps can you take to imitate John the Baptist this week?

~ 6 ~

JOHN 1:29-34

Observation & Interpretation

Read John 1:29-34 and consider the following questions.

²⁹ The next day he saw Jesus coming toward him, and said, "Behold, the Lamb of God, who takes away the sin of the world! ³⁰ This is he of whom I said, 'After me comes a man who ranks before me, because he was before me.' ³¹ I myself did not know him, but for this purpose I came baptizing with water, that he might be revealed to Israel." ³² And John bore witness: "I saw the Spirit descend from heaven like a dove, and it remained on him. ³³ I myself did not know him, but he who sent me to baptize with water said to me, 'He on whom you see the Spirit descend and remain, this is he who baptizes with the Holy Spirit.' ³⁴ And I have seen and have borne witness that this is the Son of God."

1. This passage records what happened "the next day" after the Pharisees questioned John. What happened, according to John 1:29?

2. In John 1:32–34, John the Baptist testified to an event that had happened previously, and it's been recorded for us in **Matthew 3:13-17**. Read this passage in Matthew and record your observations below.

[13] Then Jesus came from Galilee to the Jordan to John, to be baptized by him. [14] John would have prevented him, saying, "I need to be baptized by you, and do you come to me?" [15] But Jesus answered him, "Let it be so now, for thus it is fitting for us to fulfill all righteousness." Then he consented. [16] And when Jesus was baptized, immediately he went up from the water, and behold, the heavens were opened to him, and he saw the Spirit of God descending like a dove and coming to rest on him; [17] and behold, a voice from heaven said, "This is my beloved Son, with whom I am well pleased."

3. In John 1:29-34, John the Baptist shares what he saw at Jesus's baptism and what he learned during this event. List the things John the Baptist says about Jesus from John 1:29-34.

Verse 29

Verse 30

Verse 31

Verse 32

Verse 33

Verse 34

4. It is difficult to understand whether John the Baptist knew about the sacrificial trajectory of Jesus's life. So, we don't know if John the Baptist fully knew what he was prophesying when he declared Jesus was "the lamb of God who takes away the sin of the world." But on this side of the cross, we can see how this title points us to several points in God's story of redemption.

Read the following passages and <u>underline</u> and/or make observations about the role of the "lamb."

Isaiah 53:4-12

Surely he has borne our griefs
and carried our sorrows;
yet we esteemed him stricken,
smitten by God, and afflicted.
⁵ But he was pierced for our transgressions;
he was crushed for our iniquities;
upon him was the chastisement that brought us peace,
and with his wounds we are healed.
⁶ All we like sheep have gone astray;
we have turned—every one—to his own way;
and the Lord has laid on him
the iniquity of us all.
⁷ He was oppressed, and he was afflicted,
yet he opened not his mouth;
like a lamb that is led to the slaughter,
and like a sheep that before its shearers is silent,
so he opened not his mouth.
⁸ By oppression and judgment he was taken away;
and as for his generation, who considered
that he was cut off out of the land of the living,
stricken for the transgression of my people?

⁹ And they made his grave with the wicked
  and with a rich man in his death,
although he had done no violence,
  and there was no deceit in his mouth.
    ¹⁰ Yet it was the will of the Lord to crush him;
  he has put him to grief;
when his soul makes an offering for guilt,
  he shall see his offspring; he shall prolong his days;
the will of the Lord shall prosper in his hand.
¹¹ Out of the anguish of his soul he shall see and be satisfied;
by his knowledge shall the righteous one, my servant,
  make many to be accounted righteous,
  and he shall bear their iniquities.
¹² Therefore I will divide him a portion with the many,
  and he shall divide the spoil with the strong,
because he poured out his soul to death
  and was numbered with the transgressors;
yet he bore the sin of many,
  and makes intercession for the transgressors.

Exodus 12:1-28

12 The Lord said to Moses and Aaron in the land of Egypt, ² "This month shall be for you the beginning of months. It shall be the first month of the year for you. ³ Tell all the congregation of Israel that on the tenth day of this month every man shall take a lamb according to their fathers' houses, a lamb for a household. ⁴ And if the household is too small for a lamb, then he and his nearest neighbor shall take according to the number of persons; according to what each can eat you shall make your count for the lamb. ⁵ Your lamb shall be without blemish, a male a year old. You may take it from the sheep or from the goats, ⁶ and you shall keep it until the fourteenth day of this month, when the whole assembly of the congregation of Israel shall kill their lambs at twilight.

[7] "Then they shall take some of the blood and put it on the two doorposts and the lintel of the houses in which they eat it. [8] They shall eat the flesh that night, roasted on the fire; with unleavened bread and bitter herbs they shall eat it. [9] Do not eat any of it raw or boiled in water, but roasted, its head with its legs and its inner parts. [10] And you shall let none of it remain until the morning; anything that remains until the morning you shall burn. [11] In this manner you shall eat it: with your belt fastened, your sandals on your feet, and your staff in your hand. And you shall eat it in haste. It is the Lord's Passover. [12] For I will pass through the land of Egypt that night, and I will strike all the firstborn in the land of Egypt, both man and beast; and on all the gods of Egypt I will execute judgments: I am the Lord. [13] The blood shall be a sign for you, on the houses where you are. And when I see the blood, I will pass over you, and no plague will befall you to destroy you, when I strike the land of Egypt.

[14] "This day shall be for you a memorial day, and you shall keep it as a feast to the Lord; throughout your generations, as a statute forever, you shall keep it as a feast. [15] Seven days you shall eat unleavened bread. On the first day you shall remove leaven out of your houses, for if anyone eats what is leavened, from the first day until the seventh day, that person shall be cut off from Israel. [16] On the first day you shall hold a holy assembly, and on the seventh day a holy assembly. No work shall be done on those days. But what everyone needs to eat, that alone may be prepared by you. [17] And you shall observe the Feast of Unleavened Bread, for on this very day I brought your hosts out of the land of Egypt. Therefore you shall observe this day, throughout your generations, as a statute forever. [18] In the first month, from the fourteenth day of the month at evening, you shall eat unleavened bread until the twenty-first day of the month at evening. [19] For seven days

no leaven is to be found in your houses. If anyone eats what is leavened, that person will be cut off from the congregation of Israel, whether he is a sojourner or a native of the land. [20] You shall eat nothing leavened; in all your dwelling places you shall eat unleavened bread."

[21] Then Moses called all the elders of Israel and said to them, "Go and select lambs for yourselves according to your clans, and kill the Passover lamb. [22] Take a bunch of hyssop and dip it in the blood that is in the basin, and touch the lintel and the two doorposts with the blood that is in the basin. None of you shall go out of the door of his house until the morning. [23] For the Lord will pass through to strike the Egyptians, and when he sees the blood on the lintel and on the two doorposts, the Lord will pass over the door and will not allow the destroyer to enter your houses to strike you.[24] You shall observe this rite as a statute for you and for your sons forever. [25] And when you come to the land that the Lord will give you, as he has promised, you shall keep this service. [26] And when your children say to you, 'What do you mean by this service?' [27] you shall say, 'It is the sacrifice of the Lord's Passover, for he passed over the houses of the people of Israel in Egypt, when he struck the Egyptians but spared our houses.'" And the people bowed their heads and worshiped.

[28] Then the people of Israel went and did so; as the Lord had commanded Moses and Aaron, so they did.

Revelation 5

5 Then I saw in the right hand of him who was seated on the throne a scroll written within and on the back, sealed with seven seals. [2] And I saw a mighty angel proclaiming with a loud voice, "Who is worthy to open the scroll and break its seals?"[3] And no one in heaven or on earth or under the earth was able to open the scroll or to look into it, [4] and I began to weep loudly because no

one was found worthy to open the scroll or to look into it. [5] And one of the elders said to me, "Weep no more; behold, the Lion of the tribe of Judah, the Root of David, has conquered, so that he can open the scroll and its seven seals."

[6] And between the throne and the four living creatures and among the elders I saw a Lamb standing, as though it had been slain, with seven horns and with seven eyes, which are the seven spirits of God sent out into all the earth. [7] And he went and took the scroll from the right hand of him who was seated on the throne. [8] And when he had taken the scroll, the four living creatures and the twenty-four elders fell down before the Lamb, each holding a harp, and golden bowls full of incense, which are the prayers of the saints. [9] And they sang a new song, saying,

"Worthy are you to take the scroll
and to open its seals,
for you were slain, and by your blood you ransomed people for God
from every tribe and language and people and nation,
[10] and you have made them a kingdom and priests to our God,
and they shall reign on the earth."

[11] Then I looked, and I heard around the throne and the living creatures and the elders the voice of many angels, numbering myriads of myriads and thousands of thousands, [12] saying with a loud voice,

"Worthy is the Lamb who was slain,
to receive power and wealth and wisdom and might
and honor and glory and blessing!"

[13] And I heard every creature in heaven and on earth and under the earth and in the sea, and all that is in them, saying,

"To him who sits on the throne and to the Lamb
be blessing and honor and glory and might forever and ever!"

[14] And the four living creatures said, "Amen!" and the elders fell down and worshiped.

How do these passages offer insight on Christ being "the lamb of God who takes away the sin of the world"?

5. Describe the actions of the Holy Spirit in John 1:32-33.

6. Read the prophecies about Israel's promised Messiah in **Isaiah 11:1-2** and **Isaiah 61:1-3**. <u>Underline</u> what these verses say the Spirit would do to the Messiah.

11 There shall come forth a shoot from the stump of Jesse,
   and a branch from his roots shall bear fruit.
² And the Spirit of the Lord shall rest upon him,
   the Spirit of wisdom and understanding,
   the Spirit of counsel and might,
   the Spirit of knowledge and the fear of the Lord.

61 The Spirit of the Lord God is upon me,
   because the Lord has anointed me
to bring good news to the poor;
   he has sent me to bind up the brokenhearted,
to proclaim liberty to the captives,
   and the opening of the prison to those who are bound;
² to proclaim the year of the Lord's favor,
   and the day of vengeance of our God;
   to comfort all who mourn;
³ to grant to those who mourn in Zion—
   to give them a beautiful headdress instead of ashes,

the oil of gladness instead of mourning,
    the garment of praise instead of a faint spirit;
that they may be called oaks of righteousness,
    the planting of the Lord, that he may be glorified.

Considering the Isaiah passages, what do you think the Spirit's work on Jesus's baptism day was meant to show God's people?

Commentary

John 1:29

The day after the authorities questioned John, John saw Jesus coming toward him. John's followers must have been with him, and he declared, "Behold! The lamb of God who takes away the sin of the world!" It is difficult to understand what John the Baptist meant by this, as we are not sure whether John understood the sacrificial trajectory of Jesus's life. But as John the writer includes this, we see that he was declaring Jesus as the Messiah. When we hear the phrase "lamb of God who takes away the sin of the world," we recall the first Exodus where the lamb's blood was put over every house of the Israelites so that God's wrath would pass over them, and they would be delivered from slavery in Egypt. And the presence of "the lamb" continues in Biblical prophecy. The Gospel Transformation Study Bible says, "To "behold the lamb of God" is to see in Jesus the arrival of the suffering servant of Israel's prophecy (Isaiah 53:4–12) who took the punishment we deserve to give us the grace we could never earn."[19] Jesus is the Lamb of God. He, through his death and resurrection, takes away the sin of the world and delivers us from sin's slavery. Jesus brings a new Exodus, brings the end of the sacrificial system, and delivers us by His blood.

John 1:30–31

John clarifies further that Jesus is the One he spoke of on the previous day—the One who "ranks before [him] because he was before [him]." John then says for the first time, "I myself did not know him". This doesn't necessarily mean that John had never met Jesus, (they were cousins), but John seems to say that he didn't know with certainty Jesus was the Messiah until he saw the sign mentioned in verses 32–33.[20] But John knew that the reason he came and baptized with water was to prepare for Jesus to be revealed to Israel. John knew his role and position very well. He explained that his whole mission was to point to Christ, and by this testimony, Jesus is glorified.

John 1:32–33

Next, John bore witness to what he had seen as he referred to Jesus's baptism (this is recorded in Matthew 3). John says when Jesus came up out of the water, he saw the Spirit descend from heaven like a dove, and it remained on Jesus. He explained that God told him, "He on whom you see the spirit descend and remain, this is he who baptizes with the Holy Spirit." Throughout the OT, the Spirit would often fall upon important figures like prophets and kings to help them accomplish important tasks. But the prophet Isaiah predicted that God would send a deliverer to receive the Spirit and the Spirit would **remain** on Him. John is saying that Jesus is this promised deliverer.

John baptized with water as a symbol of cleansing and repentance. But God clarified that Jesus was the one who baptizes with the Holy Spirit. Jesus came so that, through the Spirit, His people would experience intimacy with God. Leon Morris says, "This had not been possible previously, for there is a quality of life that Christ and none other makes available to men. This life is a positive gift coming from the Spirit of God. Baptism with water had essentially a negative significance. It is a cleansing from... But baptism with the Spirit is positive. It is the bestowal of new life in God".[21] Through Jesus, a whole new stage of redemption was about to begin.

John 1:34

Here is the climax of John's testimony: Jesus is the chosen Son of God. God confirmed Jesus as His Son, and so John was bearing witness to the Son of God who takes away the sin of the world.

Application & Reflection

1. John declared that Jesus was "the lamb of God who takes away the sin of the world." And this truth reminds us of several places in the OT. How does understanding God's big story of Redemption help us appreciate Jesus Christ as our Messiah?

2. John the Baptist's ministry was filled with testimony of how he had seen Jesus work and what he had seen Jesus to be like. Through his words about Christ, God is glorified and Jesus is lifted up as the Messiah. How are you encouraged by the nature of John's ministry?

List some occasions in which you have seen Jesus's work.

In what ways has Jesus shown his character to you?

How could you imitate John the Baptist's ministry by sharing what God has done in your life through Christ?

3. Jesus is the "lamb of God who takes away the sin of the world". This truth should lead us to respond. Consider how this reality leads you to:

Repentance

Trust

Worship

How might you pray for a deeper response of repentance, trust, and/or worship this week?

4. Reread the song of Revelation 5, recorded below, and take some time to praise Jesus for who he is.

"And they sang a new song, saying:

"You are worthy to take the scroll
    and to open its seals,
because you were slain,
    and with your blood you purchased for God
    persons from every tribe and language and people and nation.

You have made them to be a kingdom and priests to serve our God,
    and they will reign on the earth."

Then I looked and heard the voice of many angels, numbering thousands upon thousands, and ten thousand times ten thousand. They encircled the throne and the living creatures and the elders. In a loud voice they were saying:

"Worthy is the Lamb, who was slain,
   to receive power and wealth and wisdom and strength
   and honor and glory and praise!"

Then I heard every creature in heaven and on earth and under the earth and on the sea, and all that is in them, saying:

"To him who sits on the throne and to the Lamb
   be praise and honor and glory and power,
for ever and ever!"

The four living creatures said, "Amen," and the elders fell down and worshiped."

Revelation 5:9-14

~ 7 ~

JOHN 1:35-42

Observation & Interpretation

Read John 1:35–42 and consider the following questions.

³⁵ The next day again John was standing with two of his disciples, ³⁶ and he looked at Jesus as he walked by and said, "Behold, the Lamb of God!" ³⁷ The two disciples heard him say this, and they followed Jesus. ³⁸ Jesus turned and saw them following and said to them, "What are you seeking?" And they said to him, "Rabbi" (which means Teacher), "where are you staying?" ³⁹ He said to them, "Come and you will see." So they came and saw where he was staying, and they stayed with him that day, for it was about the tenth hour. ⁴⁰ One of the two who heard John speak and followed Jesus was Andrew, Simon Peter's brother. ⁴¹ He first found his own brother Simon and said to him, "We have found the Messiah" (which means Christ). ⁴² He brought him to Jesus. Jesus looked at him and said, "You are Simon the son of John. You shall be called Cephas" (which means Peter).

1. After John the Baptist testified that Jesus was "the Lamb of God who takes away the sin of the world," people began to seek out Jesus. What happens in verses 35-37?

2. These disciples would have known that an important part of following a Rabbi was to watch how he lived in order to know him better. What do the disciples appear to be looking for according to verses 38-39?

How did Jesus respond?

3. Verse 40 tells us that one of these disciples was Andrew. What was the first thing Andrew did, according to verses 41-42?

4. Describe Jesus's actions and words towards to Peter in verse 42.

5. How does Jesus's declaration about Peter give us insight about Jesus's plans and knowledge of His disciples?

Commentary

John 1:35–37

The next day, after Jesus was confirmed by John the Baptist as "the lamb of God who takes away this sin of the world", John was standing with two of his disciples and saw Jesus again. Jesus was walking by, and John pointed him out to them. Andreas Kostenberger says, "Jesus did not call people to follow Him on a whim; rather, many of them came prepared, having heard John's (the baptist's) witness. Such a referral from one Rabbi to another is unattested in first-century Judaism."[22] But as we have already seen, John the Baptist's ministry was unique.

John 1:38–39

Jesus, who heard them following, turned to them and said, "what are you seeking?" And they answered, "Rabbi", calling him 'teacher'—"Where are you staying?" they asked. They wanted to learn from him, to be where he was and see how he lived. This was an important role of a disciple in Jesus's day; they were to see their teacher's life and understand it as intimately as they could. Jesus responded, "Come and you will see." So, they went with him, followed him, and stayed with him that day; it was about 4 o' clock in the afternoon.

John 1:40–42

One of these disciples was Andrew, Peter's brother. First, he found Simon Peter and said, "We have found the Messiah" (which means Christ). He brought him to Jesus. D.A. Carson helpfully observes that Andrew "became the first in a long line of successors who have discovered that the most common and effective Christian testimony is the private witness of a friend to a friend, brother to brother".[23] Here, Andrew models a natural method of bringing someone to Jesus so they may see his life and glory.

Jesus looked at Simon and said, "you are Simon, the son of John. You shall be called "Cephas" (John 1:42), which means Peter. "Cephas" is the Aramaic term for "rock" which is "Peter" or "Petras" in Greek. Jesus saw Simon, he knew who he would call him to be and who he would transform him into, and with this name change, Jesus declared it so. We know that God often changes the names of his people to declare their role in redemption history, (we can think of Abram to Abraham, Sarai to Sarah, and Jacob to Israel). This name change was an important part of Peter's transformation. Leon Morris explains that in this time, a name stood for the whole person and his whole personality. So, when a name is changed by God, it speaks of a new character in which the man appears. Jesus declared that Simon was a new character in his story—the "rock man". "Peter appears in all the Gospels as anything but a rock. He is impulsive, volatile, unreliable. But that was not God's last word for Peter. Jesus' words point to the change that would be wrought in him by the power of God."[24] Jesus saw Simon and told him who the Gospel would make him into.

Application & Reflection

1. Those who sought out Jesus demonstrated an eagerness to learn about His life. What might this eagerness look like for you?

What steps will you take this week to pursue an intimate knowledge of Jesus?

2. Why were Andrew's actions toward Simon Peter so important?

Who has been an "Andrew" in your life?

Take some time to thank God for the "Andrews" in your life and consider thanking them, too.

3. Is there someone in your life whom you could "bring" to Jesus to help them learn more about Him?

How might this lead you to pray today?

4. Consider the fact that Jesus intimately knew Simon; Jesus knew who he would make Simon into, and Jesus knew the role Simon would play in his Kingdom. Jesus has this knowledge of all his followers, including you. What is your response to this?

How might this lead you to pray about your service in God's kingdom?

~ 8 ~

JOHN 1:43-51

Observation and Interpretation

Read John 1:43–51 and consider the following questions.

[43] The next day Jesus decided to go to Galilee. He found Philip and said to him, "Follow me." [44] Now Philip was from Bethsaida, the city of Andrew and Peter. [45] Philip found Nathanael and said to him, "We have found him of whom Moses in the Law and also the prophets wrote, Jesus of Nazareth, the son of Joseph." [46] Nathanael said to him, "Can anything good come out of Nazareth?" Philip said to him, "Come and see." [47] Jesus saw Nathanael coming toward him and said of him, "Behold, an Israelite indeed, in whom there is no deceit!" [48] Nathanael said to him, "How do you know me?" Jesus answered him, "Before Philip called you, when you were under the fig tree, I saw you." [49] Nathanael answered him, "Rabbi, you are the Son of God! You are the King of Israel!" [50] Jesus answered him, "Because I said to you, 'I saw you under the fig tree,' do you believe? You will see greater things than these." [51] And he said to him, "Truly, truly, I say to you, you will see heaven opened, and the angels of God ascending and descending on the Son of Man."

1. According to verse 43, what happened "the next day"?

2. What do we learn about Philip and what does he do in verses 44-45?

3. What does Philip say about Jesus in verse 45?

How does Nathanael answer this?

4. Notice the instances of the phrases "see" and "saw" in verses 46-51. Record your observations below and consider: 1. How are these phrases being used? 2. Who is seeing and who is being seen?

Verse 46

Verse 47

Verse 50

Verse 51

5. What did Jesus demonstrate for Nathanael in verses 47-48?

How do you think this contributed to Nathanael 's process from cynicism to belief?

6. What does Jesus promise Nathanael in verses 50-51?

7. In Jesus's promise, Nathanael would have recognized several phrases and events (like **'Son of Man', 'Heaven opened', and "angels ascending and descending"**) from the Old Testament. Read the following scriptures in which these phrases occur and record your observations.

Genesis 28:10-14

[10] Jacob left Beersheba and went toward Haran. [11] And he came to a certain place and stayed there that night, because the sun had set. Taking one of the stones of the place, he put it under his head and lay down in that place to sleep. [12] And he dreamed, and behold, there was a ladder set up on the earth, and the top of it reached to heaven. And behold, the angels of God were ascending and descending on it! [13] And behold, the Lord stood above it and said, "I am the Lord, the God of Abraham your father and the God of Isaac. The land on which you lie I will give to you and to your offspring. [14] Your offspring shall be like the dust of the earth, and you shall spread abroad to the west and to the east and to the north and to the south, and in you and your offspring shall all the families of the earth be blessed.

Daniel 7:13-14

¹³ "I saw in the night visions,

and behold, with the clouds of heaven
    there came one like a son of man,
and he came to the Ancient of Days
    and was presented before him.
¹⁴ And to him was given dominion
    and glory and a kingdom,
that all peoples, nations, and languages
    should serve him;
his dominion is an everlasting dominion,
    which shall not pass away,
and his kingdom one
    that shall not be destroyed.

What insight do you gain about the phrases in John 1:51 from these verses?

8. Considering your observations from the previous question, what do you think Jesus may have been promising Nathaniel?

Commentary

John 1:43-45

The third day after the Pharisees questioned John the Baptist and he testified about Jesus as the Messiah, Jesus decided to go to Galilee. He found Philip and said to him, "Follow me." Philip was from Bethsaida which was also Andrew and Peter's hometown. After Philip was called, he went to find Nathaniel. He said to him, "We have found him of whom Moses in the law and also the prophets wrote, Jesus of Nazareth, the son of Joseph."

John 1:46

The Israelites had been watching and waiting for this Messiah, and he was here- but many missed the prophecies. Nazareth was never mentioned in the Old Testament, and it was a small town of no more than 2,000 people in Jesus's day. Moody tells us, "Nazareth was a town that probably gave its occupants the peculiarity of speaking with a culturally different, probably less sophisticated accent (Matthew 26:73); and it also was not listed as the "city of David", the promised birthplace of the Messiah" (Micah 5:2-4).[25] So Nathanael doubted. And this reveals what were likely some preconceived ideas about the Messiah—they did not expect him to come from a place like Nazareth. Nathanael said, "can anything good come out of Nazareth?" Philip's response to Nathanael's doubt was to tell him to "come and see" for himself. Philip had confidence that Jesus would reveal himself for who he was, so he trusted as he brought Nathaniel to see the Messiah.

John 1:47–49

As he brought him, Jesus saw Nathanael coming toward Him and demonstrated that He saw and knew him. He said, "Behold. A true Israelite indeed, in whom there is no deceit!" (John 1:47). In saying this, Jesus praised Nathanael's uprightness, honesty, and integrity. Nathanael questioned: "How do you know me?" This question shows that Jesus's brief summary of Nathanael had hit the mark.[26] But Jesus responded to him by showing him that his supernatural knowledge went even beyond this. Jesus answered him, "Before Philip called you, when you were under the fig tree, I saw you." We don't know the details of Nathanael's time under the fig tree, but what we can infer is that Jesus's acknowledgement of this moment served as a testimony of Jesus's true and supernatural sight. Morris explains, "It seems probable that Nathanael had had some outstanding experience of communion with God in the privacy of his own home, and it was this to which Jesus refers"[27]. Nathanael responded with belief: "Rabbi, you are the Son of God. You are the King of Israel!" Nathanael uses the highest terms available to him to express his worship and devotion to Jesus.

John 1:50–51

Jesus commended his faith, and encouraged Nathanael that he would see even greater things as he followed him. Jesus explains, "Truly I say to you, you will see heaven opened, and the angels of God ascending and descending on the Son of Man." In order to understand what Jesus was saying, it will help us to know that this is a combination of two Old Testament references. Genesis 28:12 records Jacob's vision when God promised him the land of his fathers. He saw angels ascending and descending on a ladder to heaven. But Jesus said Nathanael would see the angels ascending and descending on him, the "Son of Man". Jesus was saying that he was the link between heaven and earth, and the means through which heaven comes down to earth.[28]

'Son of Man' was one of Jesus's favorite titles for himself. It refers to Daniel's vision of one who has always been in heaven with the Ancient of Days and would come to earth and ascend again. Jesus Christ was the Son of Man, the one who had been with the Father from eternity past and who had come from heaven to be with his people. He was the one who would be "given dominion and glory and a kingdom that all peoples, nations, and languages should serve him; his dominion is an everlasting dominion, which shall not pass away, and his kingdom one that shall not be destroyed" (Daniel 7:14). Jesus was the Son of Man and the stairway to heaven of Jacob's vision- he was the one through whom God would keep all his promises to his people. And Jesus was saying that there would be many more times in Nathanael's future when he would see the realities and magnificence of God's gospel through Jesus Christ.

Application & Reflection

1. Philip's response to Nathanael's doubt was to bring him to Jesus so he could "come and see" him. Can you think of someone in your life who expresses doubt over the reality of Christ as the Messiah?

How might you help them to "come and see" Jesus?

How might this lead you to pray for them?

2. Nathanael was led from doubt to belief when he had an experience of Jesus **seeing** him and demonstrating supernatural knowledge and care. Reflect on a time when you witnessed God **seeing** —either you or another person.

What did you learn about God from this experience?

Describe the ways this experience impacted your faith.

3. When we "come and see" Jesus, he invites us, like Nathaniel, to explore the reality of his Glory as our Savior. How might this lead you to pray today?

~ 9 ~

JOHN 2:1-11

Observation & Interpretation

We will study Jesus's first sign in two parts. First, we will observe the events and details of the miracle, then in Lesson 9 we will study the implications from the OT and Jewish tradition.

Read John 2:1-11 and consider the following questions.

2 On the third day there was a wedding at Cana in Galilee, and the mother of Jesus was there. ²Jesus also was invited to the wedding with his disciples. ³When the wine ran out, the mother of Jesus said to him, "They have no wine." ⁴And Jesus said to her, "Woman, what does this have to do with me? My hour has not yet come." ⁵His mother said to the servants, "Do whatever he tells you."

⁶Now there were six stone water jars there for the Jewish rites of purification, each holding twenty or thirty gallons. ⁷Jesus said to the servants, "Fill the jars with water." And they filled them up to the brim. ⁸And he said to them, "Now draw some out and take it to the master of the feast." So they took it. ⁹When the master of the feast tasted the water now become wine, and did not know where it came from (though the servants who had drawn the wa-

ter knew), the master of the feast called the bridegroom [10] and said to him, "Everyone serves the good wine first, and when people have drunk freely, then the poor wine. But you have kept the good wine until now." [11] This, the first of his signs, Jesus did at Cana in Galilee, and manifested his glory. And his disciples believed in him.

1. Verse 11 tells us that this passage details Jesus's first sign. Read what **John 21:30-31** and **Mark 16:20** say about signs and consider the following questions.

[30] Now Jesus did many other signs in the presence of the disciples, which are not written in this book; [31] but these are written so that you may believe that Jesus is the Christ, the Son of God, and that by believing you may have life in his name.

[20] And they went out and preached everywhere, while the Lord worked with them and confirmed the message by accompanying signs.

What is the purpose of the "signs" that Jesus performed?

How does the purpose of Jesus's signs inform the questions we ask as we study the sign of John 2:1-11?

2. Reread John 2:1-2. What was the setting of the first miracle?

Who was present?

3. What was the problem presented in John 2:3?

4. What observations or questions do you have about the conversation between Jesus and His mother in John 2:3-5?

5. What do you observe about Mary's faith in John 2:3-5?

6. List the events of the miracle recorded in the verses below.

Verse 6

Verse 7

Verse 8

Verses 9-10

7. According to verse 11, what was the result of the miracle?

Commentary

John 2:1-5

On the third day after John was questioned by the Pharisees, there was a wedding at Cana in Galilee, and Mary, the mother of Jesus was there. Jesus and His disciples were also invited to the wedding. Mary said to Jesus, "they have no wine." Hospitality was taken very seriously in the Middle East, and this may have been a truly scandalous moment for the bridegroom's family. When the wine ran out, it would have been an embarrassment to the hosts, and Mary probably wanted to help out of compassion for the family.[29] Up to this point, Jesus had not performed a miracle, but Mary trusted in her son's resourcefulness (and it's likely she knew he could do even more than be resourceful). Jesus said, "Woman, what does this have to do with me? My hour has not yet come." In Jesus's time, "woman" was a title of respect. Scholars help us understand that the tone of this in the Greek is not as cold as it seems in the English. The NLT says, "Dear woman, that is not our problem." Her initial request was met with some opposition, but it's clear Mary did not receive this as a sharp rebuke; she knew Jesus was mindful of the bridegrooms' families' difficulty, and she trusted him to do what was necessary.[30] Mary may not have known what Jesus would do, but she trusted him. She was content to say, "your will be done". D.A Carson observes, "Mary is rebuked for presuming on the family tie yet displays faith that is perfectly content to leave the matter in Jesus's hands".[31] Mary turned to the servants and said, "Do whatever he tells you."

John 2:6-10

Here are the details and process of the miracle: there were six stone water jars for the Jewish rites of purification, each holding twenty or thirty gallons of water. The purification process is mentioned in Mark 7:1-5 – each guest of the wedding would have had to have water poured over their hands before entering (Morris, 182).[32] After the fact, Jesus used these jars to perform His miracle. He told them to fill the jars with water, and so they filled them "to the brim" (vs. 7). Then Jesus said to them, "Now draw some out and take it to the master of the feast." Josh Moody eloquently says, "He does not need time; he does not need extra ingredients; he does not perform some magic ceremony. He simply instructs the servants to do as he asks (7-8), and there is wine instead of water."[33] The master of the feast took it and tasted the water turned wine (he didn't know where it came from, but the servants knew). The master of the feast called the bridegroom and praised him for his generosity. While normally the best wine would be served at the beginning, the master declared that the hosts had saved the best wine for the end.

John 2:11

This sign manifested the glory of Jesus, the Creator of the fruit of the vine and the One able to turn water into wine. And his disciples believed in him.

Application and Reflection

1. What can we learn from Mary's faith in this passage?

How can you apply this this week?

2. What do you learn about Jesus from this passage that leads you to worship Him?

~ 10 ~

JOHN 2:1-11 (PT. 2)

Observation and Interpretation

Reread John 2:1-11 and consider the following questions.

2 On the third day there was a wedding at Cana in Galilee, and the mother of Jesus was there. ²Jesus also was invited to the wedding with his disciples. ³When the wine ran out, the mother of Jesus said to him, "They have no wine." ⁴And Jesus said to her, "Woman, what does this have to do with me? My hour has not yet come." ⁵His mother said to the servants, "Do whatever he tells you."

⁶Now there were six stone water jars there for the Jewish rites of purification, each holding twenty or thirty gallons. ⁷Jesus said to the servants, "Fill the jars with water." And they filled them up to the brim. ⁸And he said to them, "Now draw some out and take it to the master of the feast." So they took it. ⁹When the master of the feast tasted the water now become wine, and did not know where it came from (though the servants who had drawn the water knew), the master of the feast called the bridegroom ¹⁰and said to him, "Everyone serves the good wine first, and when people have drunk freely, then the poor wine. But you have kept the good wine until now." ¹¹This, the first of his signs, Jesus did at Cana

in Galilee, and manifested his glory. And his disciples believed in him.

1. Read the following verses that refer to wine in the OT and consider: what do wine and seasons of plentiful wine seem to represent?

Jeremiah 31:12

They shall come and sing aloud on the height of Zion,
    and they shall be radiant over the goodness of the Lord,
over the grain, the wine, and the oil,
    and over the young of the flock and the herd;
their life shall be like a watered garden,
    and they shall languish no more.

Hosea 14:7

[7] They shall return and dwell beneath my shadow;
    they shall flourish like the grain;
they shall blossom like the vine;
    their fame shall be like the wine of Lebanon.

Isaiah 25:6-8

[6] On this mountain the Lord of hosts will make for all peoples
    a feast of rich food, a feast of well-aged wine,
    of rich food full of marrow, of aged wine well refined.
[7] And he will swallow up on this mountain
    the covering that is cast over all peoples,
    the veil that is spread over all nations.
[8]   He will swallow up death forever;
and the Lord God will wipe away tears from all faces,
    and the reproach of his people he will take away from all the

earth,
  for the Lord has spoken.

Amos 9:13-14

[13] "Behold, the days are coming," declares the Lord,
  "when the plowman shall overtake the reaper
  and the treader of grapes him who sows the seed;
the mountains shall drip sweet wine,
  and all the hills shall flow with it.
[14] I will restore the fortunes of my people Israel,
  and they shall rebuild the ruined cities and inhabit them;
they shall plant vineyards and drink their wine,
  and they shall make gardens and eat their fruit.

Psalm 104:14-15

[14] You cause the grass to grow for the livestock
  and plants for man to cultivate,
that he may bring forth food from the earth
[15] and wine to gladden the heart of man,
oil to make his face shine
  and bread to strengthen man's heart.

2. Considering this background of wine from the OT, how do you think the original audience of this recorded sign may have understood the significance of running out of wine at a Jewish wedding and Jesus's ability to replenish that wine?

3. In John 2:6, we are given the detail that the jars Jesus used were meant for the Jewish rites of purification. Read more about those laws in **Mark 7:1-7** and record your observations.

7 Now when the Pharisees gathered to him, with some of the scribes who had come from Jerusalem, ² they saw that some of his disciples ate with hands that were defiled, that is, unwashed. ³ (For the Pharisees and all the Jews do not eat unless they wash their hands properly, holding to the tradition of the elders, ⁴ and when they come from the marketplace, they do not eat unless they wash. And there are many other traditions that they observe, such as the washing of cups and pots and copper vessels and dining couches.) ⁵ And the Pharisees and the scribes asked him, "Why do your disciples not walk according to the tradition of the elders, but eat with defiled hands?"

⁶ And he said to them, "Well did Isaiah prophesy of you hypocrites, as it is written, "'This people honors me with their lips,
   but their heart is far from me;
⁷ in vain do they worship me,
   teaching as doctrines the commandments of men.'
⁸ You leave the commandment of God and hold to the tradition of men."

4. Now, consider that Jesus turned the water from these purification jars into wine for celebration. What do you think is the significance of this?

5. How does Jesus turning the water into wine point to his glory and Kingdom work?

Commentary

R.C. Sproul reminds us that Jesus's signs "pointed not only to his person, but to his work of bringing the kingdom of God...they represented God's accreditation that Jesus was sent from Him." This is important as we study Jesus's first sign; we will keep in mind that through the wedding at Cana, Jesus is pointing toward His kingdom mission.

Jesus's miracle at Cana was a joyous sign that pointed to Him as the gracious Creator. And when we consider this sign from the angle that Jesus is the fulfillment of the Old Testament, there are even more facets of Jesus's glory to be explored. This section aims to explain the depth of the passage when understood in light of Jesus as the fulfillment of the Old Testament.

When vineyards were planted and wine was made, the Jews saw it as a gift from God that made the heart glad (Psalm 104:15). At a celebration as joyous as a wedding, for the bridegroom to run out of wine would be embarrassing, but in John's mind, it may have even been symbolic. The ESV Study Bible explains that the wedding party's depletion of wine may be seen as symbolizing the spiritual barrenness of first century Judaism, especially against the OT background that views wine as a sign of joy and God's blessing.[34] The depth of the symbolism of a lack of wine is echoed by prophets like Habakkuk and Hosea – when they spoke of a lack of wine, they described it as evidence of no celebration or joy in the land (Hosea 2:9, Habakkuk 3:16-19).

In contrast, when the prophets foretold the messianic age, they characterized it as a time when God "gives back her vineyards" and wine would flow liberally (Jeremiah 31:12, Hosea 2:15, 14:7, Amos 9:13-14). As the Kingdom of heaven breaks through, Jesus graciously gives a sign that points to His glory by turning the water into the best wine. John's point was that "the wine Jesus provides is unqualifiedly superior, as must everything be that is tied to the new, messianic age that Jesus is producing".[35]

Many scholars have also noted that Jesus produced this wine in Jewish purification jars. For the original readers, these jars represented a manifestation of the religion of Moses's law. When Jesus came, He used these vessels to turn water to wine as he replaced this religious ritual water with the wine of the gospel. C.H Dodd explains that the waterpots stand for the entire system of observance to the ceremonial law, and that this sign at Cana illustrates the doctrine of John 1:17 which says, "the law came through Moses... and grace and truth came through Jesus Christ"[36]. Andreas Kostenberger says, "Against the backdrop of the barrenness of contemporary Judaism, epitomized by the reference to Jewish purification rites, Jesus appears as the messianic bridegroom who comes to bring joy and restoration to Israel."[37] Jesus came to restore what was depleted in Israel.

In John 2:1-11, Jesus comes to a wedding as the promised Bridegroom to restore the wine, celebration, and joy to his people. Jesus is the New Covenant lawgiver who led his people out of slavery to sin and began his ministry by turning water into the best wine, all while pointing to the Messianic age when wine and celebration would flow liberally. Jesus's first miracle reminds us that he is moving toward a great wedding banquet- a"feast of rich food, a feast of well-aged wine" (Isaiah 25:6), where the Bridegroom will be united to his church in joyous marital unity. The law and its consequences came through Moses, but the greater grace, the joyous covenant blessings of celebration and feasting with God and his best wine came through Jesus Christ.

Application & Reflection

1. Jesus can restore joy to the barren through His finished work. How have you seen God restore joy to hopelessness in your life or in the life of another?

What did this event teach you about the work of Jesus?

2. Consider the fact that the work of Christ calls for rejoicing and celebration. What role does rejoicing and celebration over the work of Christ have in your life?

How might these observations lead you to pray?

3. In Jesus's time, the long waiting, barrenness, and joylessness of God's people was met with hope as Jesus promised the New Covenant through His blood. Today, we wait with expectation for Jesus to return as our Bridegroom at the wedding banquet of the Lamb where wine will flow freely and joy will be restored.

How does this parallel help you to worship Jesus as you wait for His return?

4. Consider the following verses about the restoration of joy and celebration through Christ and **take some time to pray that joy would be a mark of your Christian life.**

"You have put more joy in my heart than they have when their grain and wine abound." Psalm 4:7

"Create in me a pure heart, O God, and renew a steadfast spirit within me. Do not cast me from your presence or take your Holy Spirit from me. Restore to me the joy of your salvation and grant me a willing spirit, to sustain me." Psalm 51:10-12

"When the Lord restored the fortunes of Zion,
we were like those who dreamed.
Our mouths were filled with laughter,
our tongues with songs of joy.
Then it was said among the nations,
"The Lord has done great things for them."
The Lord has done great things for us,
and we are filled with joy.
Restore our fortunes, Lord,
like streams in the Negev.
Those who sow with tears
will reap with songs of joy.
Those who go out weeping,
carrying seed to sow,
will return with songs of joy,
carrying sheaves with them."
Psalm 126

~ 11 ~

JOHN 2:12-17

Observation and Interpretation

Read John 2:12-17 and consider the following questions.

¹² After this he went down to Capernaum, with his mother and his brothers and his disciples, and they stayed there for a few days.

¹³ The Passover of the Jews was at hand, and Jesus went up to Jerusalem. ¹⁴ In the temple he found those who were selling oxen and sheep and pigeons, and the money-changers sitting there. ¹⁵ And making a whip of cords, he drove them all out of the temple, with the sheep and oxen. And he poured out the coins of the money-changers and overturned their tables. ¹⁶ And he told those who sold the pigeons, "Take these things away; do not make my Father's house a house of trade." ¹⁷ His disciples remembered that it was written, "Zeal for your house will consume me."

1. According to verse 12, what did Jesus do after the wedding at Cana?

2. Read the following verses for some background on the Passover festival.

John 11:55

[55] Now the Passover of the Jews was at hand, and many went up from the country to Jerusalem before the Passover to purify themselves.

Deuteronomy 16:1-6

16 "Observe the month of Abib and keep the Passover to the Lord your God, for in the month of Abib the Lord your God brought you out of Egypt by night. [2] And you shall offer the Passover sacrifice to the Lord your God, from the flock or the herd, at the place that the Lord will choose, to make his name dwell there. [3] You shall eat no leavened bread with it. Seven days you shall eat it with unleavened bread, the bread of affliction—for you came out of the land of Egypt in haste—that all the days of your life you may remember the day when you came out of the land of Egypt. [4] No leaven shall be seen with you in all your territory for seven days, nor shall any of the flesh that you sacrifice on the evening of the first day remain all night until morning. [5] You may not offer the Passover sacrifice within any of your towns that the Lord your God is giving you, [6] but at the place that the Lord your God will choose, to make his name dwell in it, there you shall offer the Passover sacrifice, in the evening at sunset, at the time you came out of Egypt.

Luke 2:41

⁴¹ Now his parents went to Jerusalem every year at the Feast of the Passover.

What do these verses tell you about what it may have been like in Jerusalem during the Passover festival?

3. During the Passover, many Jews would have traveled far to come to Jerusalem and it would have been easiest to purchase their materials for sacrifices when they arrived. So, many merchants saw this as an opportunity to gather and sell the prescribed animals for sacrifice. The money changers were there to help convert coins for the required temple tax. Scholars point out that at one time, animal merchants set up their tables at the Kidron Valley on the slopes of the Mount of Olives, across from the temple. But in John 2, it seems they had moved *into* the temple and into the court of the Gentiles.

What might be the reason for the merchants moving into the temple?

4. Describe Jesus's actions in John 2:14-15.

What do you learn about his intentions from verse 16?

5. Read the following verses and <u>underline</u> what you learn about the purpose of the temple.

Exodus 25:8-9

[8] And let them make me a sanctuary, that I may dwell in their midst. [9] Exactly as I show you concerning the pattern of the tabernacle, and of all its furniture, so you shall make it.

Isaiah 56:6-8

[6] "And the foreigners who join themselves to the Lord,
   to minister to him, to love the name of the Lord,
   and to be his servants,
everyone who keeps the Sabbath and does not profane it,
   and holds fast my covenant—
[7] these I will bring to my holy mountain,
   and make them joyful in my house of prayer;
their burnt offerings and their sacrifices
   will be accepted on my altar;
for my house shall be called a house of prayer
   for all peoples."
[8] The Lord God,
   who gathers the outcasts of Israel, declares,
"I will gather yet others to him
   besides those already gathered."

Summarize the purpose of the temple.

6. Why do you think Jesus was so upset at the callous and irreverent treatment of the temple?

7. The prophecies in **Malachi 3:1-3** and **Zechariah 14:21** share more about the significance of One who would come to cleanse the temple.

3 "Behold, I send my messenger, and he will prepare the way before me. And the Lord whom you seek will suddenly come to his temple; and the messenger of the covenant in whom you delight, behold, he is coming, says the Lord of hosts. [2] But who can endure the day of his coming, and who can stand when he appears? For he is like a refiner's fire and like fullers' soap. [3] He will sit as a refiner and purifier of silver, and he will purify the sons of Levi and refine them like gold and silver, and they will bring offerings in righteousness to the Lord.

[21] And every pot in Jerusalem and Judah shall be holy to the Lord of hosts, so that all who sacrifice may come and take of them and boil the meat of the sacrifice in them. And there shall no longer be a trader in the house of the Lord of hosts on that day.

What insight do you gain from these verses?

What do you think Jesus was demonstrating about his identity as he cleansed the temple?

Commentary

John records Jesus's cleansing of the temple at the beginning of his gospel, while the other gospel writers put this event at the end. Much debate has arisen in attempt to explain this. It's possible Jesus cleansed the temple twice, (once at the beginning of his ministry and once at the end), and John places the record in the beginning of his gospel to emphasize Jesus's fulfillment of the temple.

John 2:13–14

John records that after the wedding, Jesus went down to Capernaum with his mother, his brothers, and his disciples and they stayed there a few days. The Passover Feast of the Jews was coming, and so many Jews traveled and gathered in Jerusalem to offer sacrifices and participate in the feast. When Jesus arrived, in the outer place of the temple, "the court of the gentiles" where the Gentiles could worship, there were merchants selling different animals for sacrifices. R.C Sproul explains, "At the Passover, every pilgrim was required to sacrifice an animal. However, it was very difficult for the people who came to Jerusalem from the outer villages of Israel to bring their own livestock. It was much easier for them to purchase the animals that were necessary for the sacrifices when they arrived in Jerusalem."[38] There were also money changers in the court who were there to exchange foreign currency for the approved currency so the people could pay the temple tax. D.A Carson explains, "the money changers converted money to the approved currency, charging a percentage for their service".[39] Scholars help us understand that prior to this time, the booths and tables for sales and money changing were set up significantly removed from the temple, across the Kidron Valley on the Mount of Olives. But as Jesus arrived, for the sake of convenience, these tables had been moved into the temple to the court of the

Gentiles; this impacted the peoples' ability to worship. The group most affected by this were those not born Jewish who were seeking to worship, and Jesus was deeply concerned that their worship was being impeded. Isaiah 56 records God's heart and passion for foreigners to come and gather to God's holy mountain and worship him joyfully in his house of prayer. This was an important part of God's mission that Jesus was eager to protect.

Other gospel writers seem to emphasize the dishonesty of the merchants (in Mark, Jesus calls it a "den of robbers"). But here, Jesus's concern is not their ethics, but their presence. His concern was not primarily over their business practices, but that they should not hinder the worship of his Father, and they should not be in the temple at all.

John 2:14–16

Jesus entered the temple with authority. He made a whip of chords and drove the animals out of the temple. Moody and others explain that the text doesn't imply that it was a particularly dangerous or harmful kind of whip, but it was simply meant to drive the animals out.[40] He poured out the money changers' coins and overturned their tables, demonstrating disapproval in a methodical and zealous way. Jesus turned to those who sold the pigeons and said, "Take these things away. Do not make my Father's house a house of trade." The temple was intended to be a house of prayer – a sacred place where God dwelt with his people and they could come and seek him. But the leaders in the temple had made it into a marketplace.

John 2:17

Jesus's disciples would later recall this event and remember the OT words, "Zeal for your house will consume me..." Psalm 69:9.

In this verse, David experienced a zeal for the temple that consumed him. The disciples saw David's words as pointing to Christ, the Son of David. The prophets Zechariah and Malachi also foretold a day when God would come to cleanse his temple. Zechariah 14:21 says, "And on that day, there will no longer be a merchant in the house of the Lord Almighty." And Malachi 3:1,3 says, "Then suddenly the Lord you are seeking will come into His temple...he will purify the Levites and refine them like gold and silver..." In Jesus, God is working out his purposes; Jesus is God himself who came down to cleanse the temple for his glory. These actions do not merely point to a passionate religious leader, but the Messiah who had come to lead his people out of slavery to sin and restore pure and perfect worship to his Father.

Application & Reflection

1. What does Jesus's zeal for God's house teach you about Him?

2. What do you observe from this passage about Jesus's desire to dwell with his people?

3.This passage shows that Jesus is jealous for the holiness of his house, and for his house to be accessible to those outside of it. How might this lead you to view God's house (the Church), and those outside of his house?

4. How do you think the Church today is guilty of practices that hinder others from coming into the presence of God?

5. How might this lead you to pray about your own practices of worship?

How might this lead you to pray for the unbelievers in your life?

~ 12 ~

JOHN 2:18-25

Observation and Interpretation

Read John 2:18-25 and consider the following questions.

[18] So the Jews said to him, "What sign do you show us for doing these things?" [19] Jesus answered them, "Destroy this temple, and in three days I will raise it up." [20] The Jews then said, "It has taken forty-six years to build this temple, and will you raise it up in three days?" [21] But he was speaking about the temple of his body. [22] When therefore he was raised from the dead, his disciples remembered that he had said this, and they believed the Scripture and the word that Jesus had spoken.

[23] Now when he was in Jerusalem at the Passover Feast, many believed in his name when they saw the signs that he was doing. [24] But Jesus on his part did not entrust himself to them, because he knew all people [25] and needed no one to bear witness about man, for he himself knew what was in man.

1. John 2:18 begins to tell of Pharisee's reaction to Jesus cleansing the temple. Read the following translations of John 2:18 and consider the following questions.

NIV: [18] The Jews then responded to him, "What sign can you show us to prove your authority to do all this?"

CSB: [18] So the Jews replied to him, "What sign will you show us for doing these things?"

NKJV: [18] So the Jews answered and said to Him, "What sign do You show to us, since You do these things?"

NASB: [18] The Jews then said to Him, "What sign do You show us as your authority for doing these things?"

NLT: [18] But the Jewish leaders demanded, "What are you doing? If God gave you authority to do this, show us a miraculous sign to prove it."

What did the Pharisees seem to be asking for?

Why do you think they were asking for this?

2. How does Jesus respond in verse 19?

3. According to verse 20, what did the Pharisees think Jesus was saying?

4. John admits that neither the Pharisees nor the disciples understood what Jesus was saying at the time. What commentary does John add in verses 21-22?

5. Consider your study of the purpose of the temple from the previous lesson. Look up the verses below and <u>underline</u> and/or take note of how Jesus fulfills the purpose of the temple.

Colossians 2:9-10

⁹ For in him the whole fullness of deity dwells bodily, ¹⁰ and you have been filled in him, who is the head of all rule and authority.

Hebrews 10:1-14

10 For since the law has but a shadow of the good things to come instead of the true form of these realities, it can never, by the same sacrifices that are continually offered every year, make perfect those who draw near. ² Otherwise, would they not have ceased to be offered, since the worshipers, having once been cleansed, would no longer have any consciousness of sins? ³ But in these sacrifices there is a reminder of sins every year. ⁴ For it is impossible for the blood of bulls and goats to take away sins.

⁵ Consequently, when Christ came into the world, he said,

"Sacrifices and offerings you have not desired,
   but a body have you prepared for me;
⁶ in burnt offerings and sin offerings
   you have taken no pleasure.
⁷ Then I said, 'Behold, I have come to do your will, O God,
   as it is written of me in the scroll of the book.'"

[8] When he said above, "You have neither desired nor taken pleasure in sacrifices and offerings and burnt offerings and sin offerings" (these are offered according to the law), [9] then he added, "Behold, I have come to do your will." He does away with the first in order to establish the second. [10] And by that will we have been sanctified through the offering of the body of Jesus Christ once for all.

[11] And every priest stands daily at his service, offering repeatedly the same sacrifices, which can never take away sins. [12] But when Christ[b] had offered for all time a single sacrifice for sins, he sat down at the right hand of God, [13] waiting from that time until his enemies should be made a footstool for his feet. [14] For by a single offering he has perfected for all time those who are being sanctified.

John 1:14

[14] And the Word became flesh and dwelt among us, and we have seen his glory, glory as of the only Son from the Father, full of grace and truth.

Revelation 21:22-27

[22] And I saw no temple in the city, for its temple is the Lord God the Almighty and the Lamb. [23] And the city has no need of sun or moon to shine on it, for the glory of God gives it light, and its lamp is the Lamb. [24] By its light will the nations walk, and the kings of the earth will bring their glory into it, [25] and its gates will never be shut by day—and there will be no night there. [26] They will bring into it the glory and the honor of the nations. [27] But nothing unclean will ever enter it, nor anyone who does what is detestable or false, but only those who are written in the Lamb's book of life.

6. John 2:23-25 sums up Jesus's ministry at the Passover feast. Upon what was the basis of the people's belief according to verse 23?

What was Jesus's response to this according to verses 24-25?

Commentary

John 2:18–20

After Jesus cleansed the temple, the Jews said, "What sign do you show us for doing these things?" The NLT says, "If God gave you the authority to do this, show us a miraculous sign to prove it." The Pharisees saw Jesus's actions and believed that Jesus was acting outside his authority (and as we see in Malachi 3:1-3, cleansing the temple was an act of God, the Messiah). The Pharisees were alarmed; *Why did Jesus claim to have authority over God's house? Was he claiming to be the Messiah?* So, they demanded a sign that would prove he had the authority to cleanse the temple. To this, Jesus responds, "Destroy this temple and in three days I will raise it up." The Jews did not understand the profundity of this statement, partly because they were distracted by Jesus's shocking statement about the building. The temple at the time was the one built by Herod to appease the Jews (the one that was later destroyed by the Romans in A.D 70). It was a source of Jewish pride and nationalism. They were proud of their temple and were defensive as they replied, "It has taken forty-six years to build this temple, and you will raise it in three days?" (vs. 20).

John 2:21-22

John discloses that later on, after Jesus was raised from the dead, the disciples realized he was talking about the temple of his body. Moody helpfully says, "Since the temple was the place where God's people could access the presence of God, the OT temple building was always about pointing to Jesus Himself".[41] Jesus was saying, the sign that he had come as the Messiah with the authority to cleanse the temple was this: he would raise up the temple in three days through his resurrection, and his body would replace the temple. This sign would prove that Jesus is the Messiah who had come to be the true temple and restore all worship. Jesus would be the one in whom the fullness of God dwells bodily. Jesus would be the one through whom Jew and Gentile approach the throne of grace with confidence. He would give access to God through his sacrifice so that God's people may be in his presence. The sign he would perform to prove his authority over the temple was the same sign that would prove that he *is the temple.*

Revelation 21-22 promises even more fulfillment. The Gospel Transformation Study Bible beautifully says, "By Jesus's death and resurrection, the templeless worship of the garden of Eden will once again be realized in the perfected worship of the New Heaven and New Earth. On that day, God Himself and the lamb will be the temple forever."[42] After his resurrection, the disciples remembered that he had said this, and they believed the scripture and the word that Jesus had spoken.

John 2:23-25

Verses 23-25 conclude this section and sum up Jesus's ministry thus far. Many believed in his name when they saw the signs and wonders. But Jesus, on his part, did not entrust his message to them. He knew what was in their hearts — he knew that they believed primarily because of the signs and many would fall away. Just like the sign-seeking Pharisees who had accused Jesus at the temple, they were missing the point. Morris observes, "Those who had been attracted by miracles would have been ready to try to make an earthly king of him (John 6:15). But he did not entrust himself to them. He looked for genuine conversion, not enthusiasm for the spectacular".[43] It was early in Jesus's ministry, and this section reminds us that amidst all the excitement, Jesus remained sober-minded and steadfast.

Application & Reflection

1. Jesus responds to the Pharisees' demand for a sign by foretelling the sign of his crucifixion and resurrection. Think back to the purpose of signs from your study in lesson 8.

What is the purpose of a sign?

How do you think the death and resurrection of Jesus serves as the ultimate sign?

Why do you think this sign should have been more than enough for the Pharisees?

2. Sometimes we might ask for "signs" or confirmations when life feels confusing. This isn't always a bad thing, (it isn't always like what the Pharisees were doing). However, how might Jesus's death and resurrection serve as the ultimate sign of hope and confirmation in your life?

How might you respond to this "sign" with belief and prayer today?

3. Using Revelation 21:22-27 as a prompt, take some time to praise Jesus that His death and resurrection secured His fulfillment of the

temple, and a future hope of presence and worship for those who trust in His sign.

"And I saw no temple in the city, for its temple is the Lord God the Almighty and the Lamb. And the city has no need of sun or moon to shine on it, for the glory of God gives it light, and its lamp is the Lamb. By its light will the nations walk, and the kings of the earth will bring their glory into it, and its gates will never be shut by day—and there will be no night there. They will bring into it the glory and the honor of the nations. But nothing unclean will ever enter it, nor anyone who does what is detestable or false, but only those who are written in the Lamb's book of life." Revelation 21:22-27

~ 13 ~

JOHN 3:1-8

Observation & Interpretation

Read John 3:1-8 and consider the following questions.

3 Now there was a man of the Pharisees named Nicodemus, a ruler of the Jews.[2] This man came to Jesus by night and said to him, "Rabbi, we know that you are a teacher come from God, for no one can do these signs that you do unless God is with him." [3] Jesus answered him, "Truly, truly, I say to you, unless one is born again he cannot see the kingdom of God." [4] Nicodemus said to him, "How can a man be born when he is old? Can he enter a second time into his mother's womb and be born?"[5] Jesus answered, "Truly, truly, I say to you, unless one is born of water and the Spirit, he cannot enter the kingdom of God. [6] That which is born of the flesh is flesh, and that which is born of the Spirit is spirit. [7] Do not marvel that I said to you, 'You must be born again.' [8] The wind blows where it wishes, and you hear its sound, but you do not know where it comes from or where it goes. So it is with everyone who is born of the Spirit."

1. What does John 3:1 say about Nicodemus?

2. We see Nicodemus in two other parts of John's gospel as well. Read the following verses and underline and/or take note of what you learn about Nicodemus.

John 7:45–52

[45] The officers then came to the chief priests and Pharisees, who said to them, "Why did you not bring him?" [46] The officers answered, "No one ever spoke like this man!" [47] The Pharisees answered them, "Have you also been deceived? [48] Have any of the authorities or the Pharisees believed in him? [49] But this crowd that does not know the law is accursed." [50] Nicodemus, who had gone to him before, and who was one of them, said to them, [51] "Does our law judge a man without first giving him a hearing and learning what he does?" [52] They replied, "Are you from Galilee too? Search and see that no prophet arises from Galilee."

John 19:38–42

[38] After these things Joseph of Arimathea, who was a disciple of Jesus, but secretly for fear of the Jews, asked Pilate that he might take away the body of Jesus, and Pilate gave him permission. So he came and took away his body. [39] Nicodemus also, who earlier had come to Jesus by night, came bringing a mixture of myrrh and aloes, about seventy-five pounds in weight. [40] So they took the body of Jesus and bound it in linen cloths with the spices, as is the burial custom of the Jews. [41] Now in the place where he was crucified there was a garden, and in the garden a new tomb in which no one had yet been laid. [42] So because of the Jewish day of Preparation, since the tomb was close at hand, they laid Jesus there.

3. According to John 3:2, how and under what circumstances did Nicodemus address Jesus?

What do you think this verse tells us about Nicodemus and his view of Jesus?

The text doesn't tell us explicitly what Nicodemus's goals were. Why do you think he has come to speak to Jesus?

4. Compare and contrast verse 3 with verse 5. What differences and similarities do you see?

What questions do you have about these verses?

5. Water has rich symbolism of judgment, life, and cleansing from the Old Testament that we will explore in the commentary. Both Nicodemus and John would have been aware of this symbolism. It seems here that Jesus is probably referring to an Old Testament teaching that pairs water and the Spirit together. Ezekiel 36 refers to water and the spirit when making promises about the New Covenant that Jesus was initiating. Read **Ezekiel 36:25-27** and take note of what it says about water and the Spirit.

[25] I will sprinkle clean water on you, and you shall be clean from all your uncleannesses, and from all your idols I will cleanse you. [26] And I will give you a new heart, and a new spirit I will put

within you. And I will remove the heart of stone from your flesh and give you a heart of flesh. ²⁷ And I will put my Spirit within you, and cause you to walk in my statutes and be careful to obey my rules.

Water:

Spirit:

6. Read verses 6-8 in the following translations and record your observations below.

NIV:

⁶ Flesh gives birth to flesh, but the Spirit gives birth to spirit. ⁷ You should not be surprised at my saying, 'You[b] must be born again.' ⁸ The wind blows wherever it pleases. You hear its sound, but you cannot tell where it comes from or where it is going. So it is with everyone born of the Spirit."

CSB:

⁶ Whatever is born of the flesh is flesh, and whatever is born of the Spirit is spirit. ⁷ Do not be amazed that I told you that you must be born again. ⁸ The wind blows where it pleases, and you hear its sound, but you don't know where it comes from or where it is going. So it is with everyone born of the Spirit."

NASB:

⁶ That which has been born of the flesh is flesh, and that which has been born of the Spirit is spirit. ⁷ Do not be amazed that I said to

you, 'You must be born again.' [8] The wind blows where it wishes, and you hear the sound of it, but you do not know where it is coming from and where it is going; so is everyone who has been born of the Spirit."

NLT:

[6] Humans can reproduce only human life, but the Holy Spirit gives birth to spiritual life. [7] So don't be surprised when I say, 'You must be born again.' [8] The wind blows wherever it wants. Just as you can hear the wind but can't tell where it comes from or where it is going, so you can't explain how people are born of the Spirit."

What insight did you gain that might help you understand these verses better?

7. What stands out to you about Jesus and Nicodemus's conversation so far?

What questions do you have about this conversation?

Commentary

One of the men who was seeking Jesus for his signs was named Nicodemus. He was an example of John 2:23–25 – someone who sought Jesus but did not have adequate faith yet. He was a Pharisee and a ruler of the Jews. We see later, in John 7:50, that he continued to be engaged in important discussions with the Pharisees about the identity of Jesus. And Nicodemus continued to pursue Christ even to his death—John 19:39 tells us he visited Jesus's tomb. In John 3, we see the beginnings of Nicodemus's searching.

John 3:1-2

Under the cover of night, Nicodemus comes to Jesus. He calls him Rabbi, respectfully acknowledging Jesus's status as a teacher (something we know other Pharisees did not do). He also acknowledges that there is something unique about Jesus, and that God was with him. After the signs Jesus performed, Nicodemus saw something in Jesus and he wanted to know more. But Jesus responds and says, "Truly Truly I say to you, unless one is born again, He cannot see the Kingdom of God." Nicodemus was trying to understand the Kingdom with his own abilities. Leon Morris explains, "Nicodemus would have stressed the careful observance of the Law and the traditions of the elders. For the loyal Pharisee this was the way of salvation".[44] But Jesus explained that Nicodemus could not even *see* the kingdom of God unless he was born again.

John 3:4–7

Jesus would have expected Nicodemus to grasp the significance of the new birth because of his background as a teacher of scripture, but Nicodemus does not understand at all and seems to be perplexed by the category.[45] In his doubt and amazement, Nicodemus asked, "How can a man be born when he is old? Can he enter into his mother's womb a second time and be born?" So, Jesus explained what he meant by "born again". He did not mean literally born as a baby, but he clarified, "unless one is born of water and the Spirit, he cannot enter the kingdom of God." He adds, "that which is born of the flesh is flesh, and that which is born of the Spirit is Spirit." Here, Jesus reminds him that the flesh cannot produce redemption. Neither Nicodemus's heritage as a son of Abraham nor his efforts as a spiritual leader would get him into the Kingdom of Heaven. Here, Nicodemus and his fellow Pharisees are left with no doubt that what is asked of a man is not more law, "but the power of God within him to remake him completely".[46] We are reminded of John's prologue when he says God's children are not born of the flesh or the will of man, but of God (John 1:12-13).

Nicodemus was caught up in the phrase "born again", but he was focused on the wrong concept. In verse 6, Jesus explains that the reality of being born again through the water and the Spirit could be understood through what Nicodemus already knew from the Old Testament. Nicodemus would have been reminded of Ezekiel 36:25-27 – the promise of the New Covenant in which God would "sprinkle clean water on you, and you shall be clean from all your uncleanliness"; he promised he would put his Spirit in them, breathing it into them, giving them life so they may live. To enter the Kingdom, people needed to be cleansed and resurrected by the power of God. For this, Jesus reminds Nicodemus of the Old Testament promises of the Holy Spirit.

John 3:8

In verse 8, Jesus reminds Nicodemus about the nature of the Spirit as he uses a word play between "spirit" and the "wind". The Greek word for Spirit (and also the Hebrew word) can mean "spirit", "wind", or "breath". Sproul says, "The wind blows where it wishes, sometimes very powerfully, but we cannot see it. We can only see the consequences of it, the manifestation of its power, but we don't fully know where it's coming from or where it's going."[47] The Spirit cannot be controlled or understood by humans, but it's surely at work, and we can certainly see the Spirit's effects as he pursues those who will become children of God.

Application & Reflection

1. Nicodemus was a religious leader who knew the scriptures thoroughly; he assumed this meant he was a part of the Kingdom of Heaven. But Jesus boldly and clearly tells him that unless he was born of water and the Spirit, he could not even see the kingdom of Heaven.

How are Christians today prone to rely on leadership status, traditions, heritage, or knowledge for security in God's Kingdom?

How does John 3:1–8 challenge these tendencies?

2. How is John 3:1-8 good news for both the lofty and the lowly who would seek to enter God's Kingdom?

How will you respond to this news today?

How will this news lead you to pray for others?

3. Take some time to read and reflect on the following passage about our spiritual rebirth and thank God for His salvation through Christ.

Titus 3:3–7:

"For we ourselves were once foolish, disobedient, led astray, slaves to various passions and pleasures, passing our days in malice and envy, hated by others and hating one another. But when the goodness and loving kindness of God our Savior appeared, he saved us, not because of works done by us in righteousness, but according to his own mercy, by the washing of regeneration and renewal of the Holy Spirit, whom he poured out on us richly through Jesus Christ our Savior, so that being justified by his grace we might become heirs according to the hope of eternal life."

~ 14 ~

JOHN 3:9-15

Observation & Interpretation

Read John 3:9–15 and consider the following questions.

⁹ Nicodemus said to him, "How can these things be?" ¹⁰ Jesus answered him, "Are you the teacher of Israel and yet you do not understand these things? ¹¹ Truly, truly, I say to you, we speak of what we know, and bear witness to what we have seen, but you do not receive our testimony. ¹² If I have told you earthly things and you do not believe, how can you believe if I tell you heavenly things? ¹³ No one has ascended into heaven except he who descended from heaven, the Son of Man. ¹⁴ And as Moses lifted up the serpent in the wilderness, so must the Son of Man be lifted up, ¹⁵ that whoever believes in him may have eternal life.

1. How does Nicodemus respond to Jesus's teaching in verse 9?

2. Jesus challenged Nicodemus and said Nicodemus should understand his teaching. In verse 10, why does Jesus say Nicodemus should understand?

What does this tell us about the importance of knowing the Old Testament context of Jesus's words?

3. In verses 11 and 12, Jesus reminds Nicodemus that 'they' have born witness to what they have seen, but the teachers of Israel, the Pharisees, have not received their testimony. The ESV Study Bible explains the "we" in this verse may be referring to either the trinity, "Jesus and John the Baptist, Jesus and his disciples, or an entire string of witnesses including OT prophets, John the Baptist, Jesus, and His disciples".[48] It is difficult to understand what Jesus means when he says "earthly" and "heavenly" things in verse 12, but it is likely that he is referring to the "earthly" illustrations he uses for his teaching (like birth, bread, and water) compared with the heavenly things that only he has seen and known.

Read John 3:11-12 in the following translations as you consider the context above. Then, paraphrase these verses in your own words.

NIV: [11] Very truly I tell you, we speak of what we know, and we testify to what we have seen, but still you people do not accept our testimony. [12] I have spoken to you of earthly things and you do not believe; how then will you believe if I speak of heavenly things?

NASB: [11] Truly, truly, I say to you, we speak of what we know and testify of what we have seen, and you *people* do not accept our testimony. [12] If I told you earthly things and you do not believe, how will you believe if I tell you heavenly things?

CSB: [11] Very truly I tell you, we speak of what we know, and we testify to what we have seen, but still you people do not accept our testimony. [12] I have spoken to you of earthly things and you do not believe; how then will you believe if I speak of heavenly things?

NLT: [11] I assure you, we tell you what we know and have seen, and yet you won't believe our testimony. [12] But if you don't believe me when I tell you about earthly things, how can you possibly believe if I tell you about heavenly things?

John 3:11-12 in your own words:

4. In verse 13, Jesus explains that he is the One who has authority to teach on heavenly things because he is the **Son of Man** who has been to heaven. Here, Jesus is using another OT reference. Read about the Son of Man Daniel saw in **Daniel 7:13-14** and record your observations.

[13] "I saw in the night visions, and behold, with the clouds of heaven
   there came one like a son of man,
and he came to the Ancient of Days
   and was presented before him.
[14] And to him was given dominion
   and glory and a kingdom,
that all peoples, nations, and languages
   should serve him;
his dominion is an everlasting dominion,
   which shall not pass away,
and his kingdom one
   that shall not be destroyed.

What is the significance of Jesus calling Himself the Son of Man? (What is he saying about his relationship to God?)

Why does this give him authority to teach on heavenly things?

5. What does Jesus say will happen to the Son of Man in John 3:14?

6. Jesus explains the event in verse 14 with yet another Old Testament reference. Read the account he refers to from **Numbers 21:4–9.**

[4] From Mount Hor they set out by the way to the Red Sea, to go around the land of Edom. And the people became impatient on the way. [5] And the people spoke against God and against Moses, "Why have you brought us up out of Egypt to die in the wilderness? For there is no food and no water, and we loathe this worthless food."[6] Then the Lord sent fiery serpents among the people, and they bit the people, so that many people of Israel died. [7] And the people came to Moses and said, "We have sinned, for we have spoken against the Lord and against you. Pray to the Lord, that he take away the serpents from us." So Moses prayed for the people. [8] And the Lord said to Moses, "Make a fiery serpent and set it on a pole, and everyone who is bitten, when he sees it, shall live." [9] So Moses made a bronze[c] serpent and set it on a pole. And if a serpent bit anyone, he would look at the bronze serpent and live.

Record your observations about:

The Israelites:

The Serpent on the Pole:

How does this story help us understand Jesus's statement in John 3:14-15?

Commentary

John 3:9–10

Even the teacher most acquainted with the Old Testament did not understand what Jesus was saying. Nicodemus responds, "How can these things be?" And Jesus answered him, "Are you the teacher of Israel and yet you do not understand these things?" Jesus implies that someone deeply immersed in the laws and history of the Old Covenant documents should have known what Jesus was saying. Moody explains, "While it is certainly understandable that Nicodemus was flummoxed by Jesus's teaching, Nicodemus really should have known better. He was "Israel's teacher", he was well-versed in the Jewish scriptures, and what Jesus was talking about was what the scriptures had promised would happen." The OT promised the work of the Spirit in coordination with the kingdom of God.[49] This rebuke tips us off and tells us that we also need some significant understanding of the Old Testament in order to understand Jesus's description of the New Covenant.

John 3:11–13

Verses 11 and 12 remind us that Jesus spoke of "earthly things" and used earthly examples in his teaching like water. And the Pharisees still didn't understand the testimony Jesus was giving about his kingdom when he used "earthly" illustrations and demonstrations. So, Jesus asks, how will they understand the things of heaven? God's people had been told the truth, but they had not received the truth about Jesus. Jesus says he was able to explain heavenly things: he is the Son of Man, the man Daniel saw in Daniel 7:13-14, sitting at the right hand of God. He could speak of heavenly things because he has the fullness of heavenly knowledge.[50] Jesus knew heaven, had descended from heaven, and he would ascend back to heaven.

John 3:14-15

Jesus used another OT reference to explain the way he would be "lifted up". John 3:14-15 explains that "just as Moses lifted up the serpent in the wilderness, so must the Son of Man be lifted up, that whoever believes in him may have eternal life." In Numbers 21, as Israel was headed through the wilderness to the promised land, the people failed to trust and obey God. God sent fiery serpents among them, and the serpents brought death. Israel had been condemned for their breaking of the law, and they deserved death. But they admitted their sin and called out to Moses to intercede for them. Moses interceded and called out to God, and God told him to make a fiery serpent out of bronze and lift it up on a pole. Vern Poythress observes, "The remedy for sin comes in the form of a symbol of sin and death."[51] And the symbol is lifted up so that "if a serpent bit anyone, he would look at the bronze serpent and live" (Numbers 14:9). Moses lifted up the bronze snake on a pole, and whoever looked up to the snake on a pole in faith would be healed.

Jesus interprets Numbers 14 and points to himself. As he spoke to Nicodemus, who may have thought he had already secured his way into the kingdom by his heritage and position, Jesus reminded him that Israel, too, needed saving from their condemnation through the cleansing of the water and the spirit, and through faith in a Savior from their sin. Their unbelief condemned them, and their sin deserved death. But Jesus came to intercede and to be "lifted up" on a "symbol of sin and death", the cross, so that those who would look to him in faith would receive eternal life. Nicodemus and Israel were being told to look to Jesus for their new birth just like the Israelites looked to the serpent on the pole for their physical life. D.A. Carson explains, "The Greek verb for 'lifted up'... in its four occurrences in this Gospel (cf. 8:28; 12:32, 34) always combine the notions of being physically lifted up on the cross, with the notion of exaltation."[52] In John 12:32, Jesus explains, "And I, when I am lifted up from the earth, will draw all men to myself." Moses interceded and lifted up the serpent on the pole. In doing so, he offered an opportunity for those who had been condemned to death to be given physical life. God's remedy to save His people from sin for Jesus to give up His life and be lifted up on the cross. When people look to Jesus in faith, they may be healed, not just from the physical consequence of sin, but they are healed from their condemnation and given eternal life in his name.

Application & Reflection

1. God's faithfulness to us in Christ started with His faithfulness to the Israelites and the Old Covenant. This means we can understand Jesus better in the context of the Old Testament. How is this truth challenging to you?

How does this truth encourage you?

2. Apart from God's saving work, our condition is the same as the Israelites who were writhing in pain from poisonous snake bites.

What does Jesus's teaching about Numbers 21 teach you about your need for a Savior?

3. What does Jesus's teaching about Numbers 21 teach you about the cross?

~ 15 ~

JOHN 3:16-21

Observation & Interpretation

Read John 3:16-21 and consider the following questions.

[16] "For God so loved the world, that he gave his only Son, that whoever believes in him should not perish but have eternal life. [17] For God did not send his Son into the world to condemn the world, but in order that the world might be saved through him. [18] Whoever believes in him is not condemned, but whoever does not believe is condemned already, because he has not believed in the name of the only Son of God. [19] And this is the judgment: the light has come into the world, and people loved the darkness rather than the light because their works were evil. [20] For everyone who does wicked things hates the light and does not come to the light, lest his works should be exposed. [21] But whoever does what is true comes to the light, so that it may be clearly seen that his works have been carried out in God."

1. After comparing the work of the Son of Man to the serpent lifted on the pole in Numbers 21:4-9, Jesus explained the motivation of God's work in John 3:16. According to John 3:16:

What did God do?

What was his motivation?

What is the intended result for God's people?

2. Review Numbers 21:4-9 alongside John 3:16 as you fill out the chart below.

	Numbers 21:4-9	John 3:16
The condition of humanity apart from intervention		
The Healer/Solution		
The Posture & act required of humanity		
Result		

How does this comparison help you better understand God's mission through Christ?

3. According to John 3:17, why did God **not** send his Son into the world and why **did** he send his Son into the world?

4. Verses 18-21 compare two kinds of people. Fill out the chart below with your observations about two those who believe and those who don't believe.

Those Who Believe	Those Who Don't Believe
Verse 18	
Verse 19	
Verse 20	
Verse 21	

5. Read the following different translations of **John 3:20-21**. Then, paraphrase these verses in your own words.

NIV: [20] Everyone who does evil hates the light, and will not come into the light for fear that their deeds will be exposed. [21] But whoever lives by the truth comes into the light, so that it may be seen plainly that what they have done has been done in the sight of God.

CSB: [20] For everyone who does evil hates the light and avoids it, so that his deeds may not be exposed. [21] But anyone who lives by the truth comes to the light, so that his works may be shown to be accomplished by God."

NASB: [20] For everyone who does evil hates the Light, and does not come to the Light, so that his deeds will not be exposed. [21] But the one who practices the truth comes to the Light, so that his deeds will be revealed as having been performed in God."

NKJV: [20] For everyone practicing evil hates the light and does not come to the light, lest his deeds should be exposed. [21] But he who does the truth comes to the light, that his deeds may be clearly seen, that they have been done in God."

NLT: [20] All who do evil hate the light and refuse to go near it for fear their sins will be exposed. [21] But those who do what is right come to the light so others can see that they are doing what God wants.

John 3:20-21 paraphrased in your own words:

Commentary

John 3:16

After Jesus explains God's mission, He describes God's heart and purpose in John 3:16. God so loved the world, the fallen humanity and cosmos, that he gave his one and only Son. The words "one and only" emphasize the extravagance of his gift. Leon Morris elaborates on the beauty of this verse: "The Jew was ready enough to think of God as loving Israel, but no passage appears to be cited in which any Jewish writer maintains that God loved the world. It is a distinctively Christian idea that God's love is wide enough to embrace all mankind. His love is not confined to any national group or any spiritual elite. It is a love that proceeds from the fact that He is love (1 John 4:8,16). It is His nature to love. He loves men because He is the kind of God He is. John tells us that His love is shown in the gift of His Son."[53] God gave Jesus so that whoever believes in the Son, would not perish, but have eternal life. R.C Sproul says, "It's the good news that snake bitten people, people infected by a poison that goes to the depth of their souls, can look to the cross and find salvation."[54] Whoever believes in Christ lifted up on the cross will be rescued from their sin and given eternal life.

John 3:17–18

God sent his one and only Son into the world, not to condemn the world, but in order that they may be saved by the work of the Son. Whoever believes in him is not condemned, because he took the condemnation for them. But whoever does not believe is condemned (their inability to uphold the law has condemned them already). Moody says, "Our condemnation remains if we do not believe in Jesus (v.18) because, like the Israelites in the wilderness, we have disobeyed God and complained against his good provision, and we deserve his just condemnation."[55] Apart from hope in Christ lifted up, they are condemned, because in their sinful state they can not uphold the law, and they are rejecting the one who was condemned for them.

John 3:19–20

Humanity was already in need of a Savior before God's Son came on his saving mission, and this person compounds his or her guilt by not believing in the name of that Son.[56] What is the judgment against them? It's described for us in metaphorical terms: the light, (Christ), has come into the world, and people loved the darkness rather than the light, because their works were evil. Sproul says apart from Christ we are "attracted to hiding". All who do evil hate the light and refuse to go near it; they don't want their hearts and deeds exposed, so they hide from the light.

John 3:21

But whoever does what is true, who depends on Christ and has been given a new heart, they long for the light. God's children want to be seen by him and for their works to glorify him.

Application & Reflection

1. What does it mean to you that God did not send his Son to condemn the world, but to save his people through him?

How might this truth inform the way you pray for unbelievers in your life?

2. Consider the characteristics of one who "comes to the light" (vs. 21). How do the lives of people who live in the light bring glory to God?

3. We "live in the light" when we live a life of repentance, obedience, and worship before God and others. How might this call to live "in the light" lead you to pray for God's work in and through you?

How might this lead you to pray for God's work in your church and your community?

4. What is your reaction to, as Leon Morris explains, the "distinctively Christian idea" that God's love is wide enough to embrace all mankind?

5. Take some time to praise and thank God for the gracious gift of the Gospel as it is explained in John 3:16-17.

"For God so loved the world, that he gave his only Son, that whoever believes in him should not perish but have eternal life. For God did not send his Son into the world to condemn the world, but in order that the world might be saved through him."

~ 16 ~

JOHN 3:22-30

Observation & Interpretation

Read John 3:22-30 and consider the following questions.

²² After this Jesus and his disciples went into the Judean countryside, and he remained there with them and was baptizing. ²³ John also was baptizing at Aenon near Salim, because water was plentiful there, and people were coming and being baptized ²⁴ (for John had not yet been put in prison).
²⁵ Now a discussion arose between some of John's disciples and a Jew over purification. ²⁶ And they came to John and said to him, "Rabbi, he who was with you across the Jordan, to whom you bore witness—look, he is baptizing, and all are going to him." ²⁷ John answered, "A person cannot receive even one thing unless it is given him from heaven. ²⁸ You yourselves bear me witness, that I said, 'I am not the Christ, but I have been sent before him.' ²⁹ The one who has the bride is the bridegroom. The friend of the bridegroom, who stands and hears him, rejoices greatly at the bridegroom's voice. Therefore this joy of mine is now complete. ³⁰ He must increase, but I must decrease."

1. After the conversation with Nicodemus, Jesus and his disciples started moving from Jerusalem to the Judean countryside. What were they doing and who was there according to John 3:22-24?

2. We are not told the details of the conversation in verse 25, but apparently it prompted John the Baptist's disciples to have questions about his ministry. What do they tell John in John 3:26?

What seems to be their concern?

3. What is John's answer according to 3:27-28?

Why do you think he responded this way?

4. What is the illustration John uses in verse 29?

How does this help you understand John's view of ministry?

5. What is John's summary according to John 3:30?

6. Given this information, summarize John's vision and approach to ministry in your own words.

Commentary

John 3: 22–24

After Jesus's conversation with Nicodemus, he and his disciples went to the Judean countryside. John had been baptizing with a baptism of repentance (in Jewish tradition, ritual cleansing baptisms were an important part of purification). Jesus partnered with John in preparing them for the kingdom by encouraging this repentance and baptism. At this point, John was baptizing at Aenon near Salim because there was plenty of water there.

John 3:23–30

A discussion came up between some of John's disciples and a Jew over purification. Whatever it was, the conversation prompted them to go to John to say, "Rabbi, he who was with you across the Jordan, to whom you bore witness, look, he is baptizing, and all are going to him." They had heard John testify that Jesus was the lamb of God who takes away the sin of the world, but they were still confused. What was John's role in all this? If all were leaving John's ministry and going to Jesus, was John upset? What were John's disciples supposed to do? John answers, "a person can not receive one thing unless it is given from heaven." Both John's ministry and Jesus's ministry were under heaven's rule. Both Jesus and John received their assignments from God, and John was content with his. John grasping to try to get disciples back would have done nothing, even if that was what he had wanted to do. John expanded and reminded them that he had already explained that he was not the

Christ. His God-given role was to be sent before Jesus to prepare the way.

Then, John illustrated his relationship to Jesus with the image of a wedding. He explained that he, John the Baptist, was like the best man to the groom, Jesus. The NLT translates verse 29, "It is the bridegroom who marries the bride, and the bridegroom's friend is simply glad to stand with him and hear his vows. Therefore, I am filled with joy at his success." Carson helps us understand that at a Judean wedding at that time, the best man or "bridegroom's friend" would have been in charge of organizing the details and presiding over the wedding.[57] And Morris adds that "in particular, it was [the best-man] who brought the bride to the bridegroom."[58] John's job was to serve, prepare, support the Bridegroom, and bring the bride to her Bridegroom. Jesus, the true bridegroom, had come for his bride, the people of God. The Old Testament uses this illustration too; prophets like Isaiah and Hosea used the imagery of God as a faithful husband pursuing Israel as his bride (Isaiah 62:4–5, Jeremiah 2:2, Hosea 2:16–20). God's pursuing love for Israel culminated in this day when the bridegroom was made flesh in Jesus Christ. People were leaving John and going to Jesus. It was clearly upsetting to John's disciples, but John, like a best man, was overjoyed this day had come–it was all about Jesus. He rejoiced at the Bridegroom's voice. Jesus had come to betroth himself to his bride, and the application for John was simple: Jesus must increase, but John must decrease.

Application & Reflection

1. John the Baptist's disciples saw that John was losing followers and they were concerned. Their ministry was fading, and they felt it was a problem. Sometimes believers can look at other churches or ministries' success and feel similarly. How have you seen competition and comparison between churches and ministries be harmful?

Do you see this in your own life and context?

2. John offers the antidote to the anxiety of ministry comparison with the assertion that no one can receive any ministry unless it is from God. He knew his God-given role and he embraced it. How is this attitude a remedy to ministry competition?

How might this wisdom apply to your church and/or ministry?

How might this lead you to pray today?

3. What is your reaction to the wedding illustration?

How does viewing yourself as a "best man" in relation to Jesus bring us joy in serving him?

4. Take some time to reflect on John 3:30, "He must increase, but I must decrease." Why do you think this is such a valuable perspective for faith, life, and ministry?

Is there anything hindering you from this perspective and joy?

5. Take some time to pray for a John 3:30 perspective for your own life, ministry, and circumstances.

    1.

~ 17 ~

JOHN 3:31-36 AND CONCLUSION

Observation & Interpretation

Read John 3:31-36 and consider the following questions

[31] He who comes from above is above all. He who is of the earth belongs to the earth and speaks in an earthly way. He who comes from heaven is above all. [32] He bears witness to what he has seen and heard, yet no one receives his testimony. [33] Whoever receives his testimony sets his seal to this, that God is true. [34] For he whom God has sent utters the words of God, for he gives the Spirit without measure. [35] The Father loves the Son and has given all things into his hand. [36] Whoever believes in the Son has eternal life; whoever does not obey the Son shall not see life, but the wrath of God remains on him.

1. As Chapter 3 concludes, John the Baptist sums up his ministry philosophy and points back to many principles we have learned about Jesus in chapters 1-3. He starts by expanding on why Jesus must increase, and John must decrease (John 3:30).

What is the reason according to verse 31?

2. Look back at John 3:11-13. There we learned that Jesus is the only one who can speak about heavenly things because he is the one who has been to heaven and has descended from heaven. How does verse John 3:31 expand upon what you learned in John 3:11-13?

3. Reread John 3:32-33. What was peoples' response to the testimony of Jesus?

According to verse 33, if one does receive the testimony of Jesus, what are they affirming or "setting their seal" on?

5. As we study John 3:31-36, write the characteristics described of the following kinds of people:

He who is of the earth (31):

He who comes from above; "he whom God has sent" (31, 34):

The one who "receives his testimony" and "believes" (33, 36):

The one who does not receive the testimony and "does not obey" (36):

What insight did you gain from this exercise?

Commentary & Conclusion

In his last statements of the book, John the Baptist explains in detail why Jesus must become greater: Jesus is God—he alone is from heaven and is above all.

John 3:31-32

John ends chapter 3 with John the Baptist's statement about Jesus and his forthcoming ministry. These verses bring together several themes from chapter 3, and also our whole study of John 1-3. John the Baptist has already explained who he was in relation to Jesus, and here, he shifts the focus completely to Jesus. D.A Carson reminds us, "Inevitably, [John] speaks as one from the earth: he called the people to repentance and baptism in water, but he could not reveal heavens counsels, nor could he offer regeneration from above, or the long-promised renewal of water and the spirit."[59] Jesus is from heaven, and the differences between Jesus and those he speaks to come from the fact that Jesus is from heaven and speaks in a heavenly way. Jesus speaks the truth about what he has seen and heard, and about the things of God. The reason people do not receive him is because they are earthly.

John 3:33–34

But whoever accepts Jesus's witness "sets his seal" on the proposition that God is true. Leon Morris explains, "The seal was used a great deal in antiquity when there were many who could not read. A design imprinted by a seal conveyed a clear message even to the illiterate. Great men used distinctive seals which stamped articles as belonging to them. The seal came to be used not only to denote ownership, but to authenticate, to give a man's personal guarantee (245).[60] John the Baptist was saying that when someone accepts the words of Jesus and the truth about who he is, that person is "setting his seal" or his mark of ownership on the fact that *God is true. They are saying that God's true message is revealed in the person of Jesus Christ.* Jesus speaks the words of God. God has given him his Spirit—Jesus is the one whom God's Spirit rests. The Spirit of God is given to Jesus "without measure" or as the NLT says, "without limit". **And so, to believe the true words of Jesus is to believe the true words of God.**

John 3:35–36

The Father gives Jesus the Spirit in this way because he loves the Son. They are in complete unity, and the Father has given all things into his hand. This ministry belongs to Christ, as the Father is doing all things for his glory in the exaltation of his Son. So, "Whoever believes in the Son has eternal life; whoever does not believe in the Son shall not see life. But the wrath of God remains on Him." John ends his testimony in Chapter 3 with the truth of the gospel. There are two choices: believe and receive life, disobey, and you will not see life.

Conclusion

In John 1-3, John has given testimony that Jesus is the revelation of God, the Word of God made flesh, and the one who rested in unity and intimacy with the Father (John 1:1, 14-18). He is the One whom all things are created, and he demonstrated this in his ability to turn water into the best wine, exchanging barrenness for Messianic joy and celebration (John 1:3, John 2:1-11). He came to his own, and his own did not receive him; the religious leaders rejected his authority, but Jesus demonstrated that he had authority over God's house, the temple, and he would restore the temple through his resurrection (John 1:11, 2:13-22).

And to those who did receive him, like John the Baptist, Philip, Andrew, Nathaniel, and Peter, he revealed himself as "Lamb of God who takes away the sin of the world", the Messiah, the stairway to heaven, and the God who sees and knows who we will be by the power of the Gospel. They believed in his name and were given the right to become children of God (John 1:12-13, John 1:29-42). Jesus does this by being the bringer of the New Covenant. For the law and old covenant came through Moses, but the grace and truth, and the promised renewal and cleansing of the Holy Spirit comes through the New Covenant of Jesus Christ (John 1:17, John 3:1-8).

Later, John will testify to the fulfillment of Jesus's promise. Jesus was indeed lifted up on a cross just like the serpent on the pole. God so loved the world that he gave his only begotten son so that whoever believes in him should not perish but have eternal life in him (John 3:9–16). John the Baptist demonstrates how we might respond... we are to "become less" as we behold and rejoice at the beautiful reality of who Jesus is. But as R.C Sproul reminds us, "We are invited to the wedding not simply as friends of the Bridegroom or as friends of the bride — we are the bride."[61] Jesus came to his own, the Church. Now John reminds us as he closes John 3, "believe in him and receive life" (John 3:36).

Application & Reflection

1. What did you learn from this study about John the Baptist's ministry and what it can teach us about our own ministries?

2. What did you learn from this study about the divinity of Jesus?

3. What did you learn about the ways Jesus's divinity is connected to his fulfillment of the Old Testament?

How does this inform the way you might read and understand the Old Testament?

4. What does it mean to you that for those who believe, they are given eternal life in Christ?

5. As you reflect on your time in this study, read the prologue of John (John 1:1-18) one more time. The prologue nicely outlines many things we studied like Jesus's origins from heaven (1-5), the witness of John the Baptist (6-8, 15), man's response to Jesus (9-13), and Jesus's fulfillment of the Old Testament (14-18).

1 In the beginning was the Word, and the Word was with God, and the Word was God. [2] He was in the beginning with God. [3] All things were made through him, and without him was not any thing made that was made. [4] In him was life,[a] and the life was the light of men. [5] The light shines in the darkness, and the darkness has not overcome it.

[6] There was a man sent from God, whose name was John. [7] He came as a witness, to bear witness about the light, that all might believe through him. [8] He was not the light, but came to bear witness about the light.

[9] The true light, which gives light to everyone, was coming into the world. [10] He was in the world, and the world was made through him, yet the world did not know him. [11] He came to his own, and his own people did not receive him. [12] But to all who did receive him, who believed in his name, he gave the right to become children of God, [13] who were born, not of blood nor of the will of the flesh nor of the will of man, but of God.

[14] And the Word became flesh and dwelt among us, and we have seen his glory, glory as of the only Son from the Father, full of grace and truth. [15] (John bore witness about him, and cried out, "This was he of whom I said, 'He who comes after me ranks before me, because he was before me.'") [16] For from his fullness we have all received, grace upon grace. [17] For the law was given through Moses; grace and truth came through Jesus Christ. [18] No one has ever seen God; the only God, who is at the Father's side, he has made him known.

6. Write down a few things that were helpful or memorable to you from this study.

What do you want to remember about Jesus's nature and character from this study?

7. Take some time to pray over the prologue and the characteristics of Jesus that you recorded, that you would know them more deeply, be changed by them, and share the news of Jesus with others for the Glory of God.

End Notes

1. Outline taken from D.A. Carson: D.A. Carson, *The Gospel According to John*. The Pillar New Testament Commentary Series. Edited by D.A. Carson. (Grand Rapids, Michigan, William B. Eerdmans Publishing Company, 1991). ↑

2. Michael Kruger, *Gospels,* Reformed Theological Seminary. Lecture Handout. ↑

3. Josh Moody, *John 1-12 For You*. God's Word For You Series. (The Good Book Company, 2017), 21. ↑

4. D.A Carson, *The Gospel According to John*. The Pillar New Testament Commentary Series. Edited by D.A. Carson. (Grand Rapids, Michigan, William B. Eerdmans Publishing Company, 1991). 115. ↑

5. Leon Morris, *The Gospel According to John*. The New International Commentary on the New Testament. (Grand Rapids, Michigan, William B. Eerdmans Publishing Company, 1971), 79. ↑

6. Leon Morris, *The Gospel According to John*. The New International Commentary on the New Testament. (Grand Rapids, Michigan, William B. Eerdmans Publishing Company, 1971), 84. ↑

7. Andreas Kostenberger, Commentary on John, The Gospel Coalition Commentaries. https://www.thegospelcoalition.org/commentary/john/ ↑

8. *The Gospel According to John*. The New International Commentary on the New Testament. (Grand Rapids, Michigan, William B. Eerdmans Publishing Company, 1971). ↑

9. Andreas Kostenberger, Commentary on John, The Gospel Coalition Commentaries. https://www.thegospelcoalition.org/commentary/john/ ↑

10. D.A. Carson, *The Gospel According to John*. The Pillar New Testament Commentary Series. Edited by D.A. Carson. (Grand Rapids, Michigan, William B. Eerdmans Publishing Company, 1991), 129. ↑

11. Andreas Kostenberger, *Signs of the Messiah: An Introduction to John's Gospel,* (Bellingham, Washington: Lexham Press, 2021) eBook Collection (EBSCOhost). ↑

12. ESV Study Bible (Wheaton, Crossway, 2008). ↑

13.   Leon Morris, *The Gospel According to John.* The New International Commentary on the New Testament. (Grand Rapids, Michigan, William B. Eerdmans Publishing Company, 1971),112. ↑

14.   D.A Carson, *The Gospel According to John.* The Pillar New Testament Commentary Series. Edited by D.A. Carson. (Grand Rapids, Michigan, William B. Eerdmans Publishing Company, 1991), 142. ↑

15.   Ibd., 145. ↑

16.   R.C Sproul, *John: An Expositional Commentary,* R.C Sproul Expositional Commentary Series. (Ligonier Ministries, 2019). Kindle Edition. ↑

17.   The Gospel Transformation Study Bible (ESV). (Wheaton, IL: Crossway Publishing, 2018). ↑

18.   R.C Sproul, *John: An Expositional Commentary.* R.C Sproul Expositional Commentary Series. (Ligonier Ministries, 2019). Kindle Edition. ↑

19.   The Gospel Transformation Study Bible (ESV). (Wheaton, IL: Crossway Publishing, 2018) ↑

20.   ESV Study Bible (Wheaton, Crossway, 2008). ↑

21.   Leon Morris, *The Gospel According to John.* The New International Commentary on the New Testament. (Grand Rapids, Michigan, William B. Eerdmans Publishing Company, 1971), 153. ↑

22.   Andreas Kostenberger, Commentary on John, The Gospel Coalition Commentaries. https://www.thegospelcoalition.org/commentary/john/ ↑

23.   D.A Carson, *The Gospel According to John.* The Pillar New Testament Commentary Series. Edited by D.A. Carson. (Grand Rapids, Michigan, William B. Eerdmans Publishing Company, 1991), 85. ↑

24.   Leon Morris, *The Gospel According to John.* The New International Commentary on the New Testament. (Grand Rapids, Michigan, William B. Eerdmans Publishing Company, 1971), 167. ↑

25.   Josh Moody. *John 1-12 For You.* God's Word For You Series. (The Good Book Company, 2017), ↑

26.   D.A Carson, *The Gospel According to John.* The Pillar New Testament Commentary Series. Edited by D.A. Carson. (Grand Rapids, Michigan, William B. Eerdmans Publishing Company, 1991), 180. ↑

27.   Leon Morris, *The Gospel According to John.* The New International Commentary on the New Testament. (Grand Rapids, Michigan, William B. Eerdmans Publishing Company, 1971), 167. ↑

28.   Ibd.. 171. ↑

29.   R.C Sproul, *John: An Expositional Commentary.* R.C Sproul Expositional Commentary Series. (Ligonier Ministries, 2019). Kindle Edition. ↑

30.   Leon Morris, *The Gospel According to John.* The New International Commentary on the New Testament. (Grand Rapids, Michigan, William B. Eerdmans Publishing Company, 1971), 182. ↑

31. D.A. Carson, *The Gospel According to John*. The Pillar New Testament Commentary Series. Edited by D.A. Carson. (Grand Rapids, Michigan, William B. Eerdmans Publishing Company, 1991), 170. ↑

32. Leon Morris, *The Gospel According to John*. The New International Commentary on the New Testament. (Grand Rapids, Michigan, William B. Eerdmans Publishing Company, 1971), 182. ↑

33. Josh Moody. *John 1-12 For You*. God's Word For You Series. (The Good Book Company, 2017), 43. ↑

34. ESV Study Bible (Wheaton, Crossway, 2008), 2023 ↑

35. D.A Carson, *The Gospel According to John*. The Pillar New Testament Commentary Series. Edited by D.A. Carson. (Grand Rapids, Michigan, William B. Eerdmans Publishing Company, 1991), 170-171. ↑

36. C.H. Dodd. *The Interpretation of the Fourth Gospel.* (London: Cambridge University Press, 1965), 299. ↑

37. Andreas Kostenberger, Commentary on John, The Gospel Coalition Commentaries. https://www.thegospelcoalition.org/commentary/john/ ↑

38. R.C Sproul, *John: An Expositional Commentary.* R.C Sproul Expositional Commentary Series. (Ligonier Ministries, 2019). Kindle Edition. ↑

39. D.A. Carson, *The Gospel According to John*. The Pillar New Testament Commentary Series. Edited by D.A. Carson. (Grand Rapids, Michigan, William B. Eerdmans Publishing Company, 1991), 178. ↑

40. Josh Moody. *John 1-12 For You*. God's Word For You Series. (The Good Book Company, 2017), 50. ↑

41. Josh Moody. *John 1-12 For You*, God's Word For You Series, (The Good Book Company, 2017), 48. ↑

42. The Gospel Transformation Study Bible (ESV), (Wheaton, IL: Crossway Publishing, 2018) ↑

43. Leon Morris, *The Gospel According to John*. The New International Commentary on the New Testament. (Grand Rapids, Michigan, William B. Eerdmans Publishing Company, 1971), 207. ↑

44. Leon Morris, *The Gospel According to John*. The New International Commentary on the New Testament. (Grand Rapids, Michigan, William B. Eerdmans Publishing Company, 1971), 209. ↑

45. D.A. Carson, *The Gospel According to John*. The Pillar New Testament Commentary Series. Edited by D.A. Carson. (Grand Rapids, Michigan, William B. Eerdmans Publishing Company, 1991), 187. ↑

46. Leon Morris, *The Gospel According to John*. The New International Commentary on the New Testament. (Grand Rapids, Michigan, William B. Eerdmans Publishing Company, 1971), 209. ↑

47. R.C Sproul, *John: An Expositional Commentary.* R.C Sproul Expositional Commentary Series, (Ligonier Ministries, 2019). Kindle Edition. ↑

48. ESV Study Bible (Wheaton, Crossway, 2008), 2025. ↑

49. Josh Moody. *John 1-12 For You*. God's Word For You Series. (The Good Book Company, 2017), 59. ↑

50. Leon Morris, *The Gospel According to John*. The New International Commentary on the New Testament. (Grand Rapids, Michigan, William B. Eerdmans Publishing Company, 1971), 201. ↑

51. Vern S. Poythress, *Biblical Typology: How the Old Testament Points to Christ, His Church, and the Consummation*. (Wheaton: Crossway, 2024), 23. ↑

52. D.A. Carson, *The Gospel According to John*. The Pillar New Testament Commentary Series. Edited by D.A. Carson. (Grand Rapids, Michigan, William B. Eerdmans Publishing Company, 1991), 201. ↑

53. Leon Morris, *The Gospel According to John*. The New International Commentary on the New Testament. (Grand Rapids, Michigan, William B. Eerdmans Publishing Company, 1971), 229. ↑

54. R.C Sproul, *John: An Expositional Commentary*. R.C Sproul Expositional Commentary Series. (Ligonier Ministries, 2019). Kindle Edition. ↑

55. Josh Moody. *John 1-12 For You*. God's Word For You Series. (The Good Book Company, 2017). ↑

56. D.A. Carson, *The Gospel According to John*. The Pillar New Testament Commentary Series. Edited by D.A. Carson. (Grand Rapids, Michigan, William B. Eerdmans Publishing Company, 1991), 207. ↑

57. D.A. Carson, *The Gospel According to John*. The Pillar New Testament Commentary Series. Edited by D.A. Carson. (Grand Rapids, Michigan, William B. Eerdmans Publishing Company, 1991), 211. ↑

58. Leon Morris, *The Gospel According to John*. The New International Commentary on the New Testament. (Grand Rapids, Michigan, William B. Eerdmans Publishing Company, 1971), 241. ↑

59. D.A. Carson, *The Gospel According to John*. The Pillar New Testament Commentary Series. Edited by D.A. Carson. (Grand Rapids, Michigan, William B. Eerdmans Publishing Company, 1991). ↑

60. Leon Morris, *The Gospel According to John*. The New International Commentary on the New Testament. (Grand Rapids, Michigan, William B. Eerdmans Publishing Company, 1971).

Bibliography

ESV Study Bible. Wheaton, IL: Crossway Publishing, 2008.

The Gospel Transformation Study Bible (ESV). Wheaton, IL: Crossway Publishing, 2018.

Holy Bible, New International Version Grand Rapids, MI: Zondervan, 1973.

Holy Bible, New Living Translation. Carol Stream, IL: Tyndale, 1996.

Carson, D.A. *The Gospel According to John*. PNTC. Grand Rapids, MI: Eerdmans, 1991.

Dodd, C.H. *The Interpretation of the Fourth Gospel*. Cambridge: Cambridge University Press, 1965.

Glasson, T. Francis. *Moses in the Fourth Gospel: Studies in Biblical Theology*. First Series No. 40. 1963; repr., Eugene: Wipf and Stock Publishers, 2009.

Kostenberger, Andreas. *Commentary on John*, The Gospel Coalition Commentaries. https://www.thegospelcoalition.org/commentary/john/

Kostenberger, Andreas. *Signs of the Messiah: An Introduction to John's Gospel*, Bellingham, Washington: Lexham Press, 202. eBook Collection (EBSCOhost).

Ladd, George Eldon. *A Theology of the New Testament*. Rev. ed. Grand Rapids, MI: Eerdmans, 1993.

Lee, Dorothy. "The Significance of Moses in the Gospel of John." Australian Biblical Review 63, (2015): 52-66.

Loader, William. "The Significance of John 1:14-18 for Understanding John's Approach to Law and Ethics." The Review of Rabbinic Judaism, 19 (2016): 194-201.

Maronde. Christopher A. "Moses in the Gospel of John." Concordia Theological Quarterly 77, no. 1 (April 2013): 23-44.

Moody, Josh. *John 1-12 For You*. God's Word For You Series. The Good Book Company, 2017.

Morris, Leon. *The Gospel According to John*. NICNT. Grand Rapids, MI: Eerdmans, 1995.

Poythress, Vern S. *Biblical Typology: How the Old Testament Points to Christ, His Church, and the Consummation*. Wheaton, IL: Crossway, 2024.

Smith Robert H. "Exodus Typology in the Fourth Gospel." Journal of Biblical Literature 81, no, 4 (Dec 1962).

Sproul, R.C. *John: An Expositional Commentary*. R.C Sproul Expositional Commentary Series. Ligonier Ministries, 2019.

Trench, Robert. *The Miracles of our Lord*, New York: Appleton, 1886.

www.ingramcontent.com/pod-product-compliance
Lightning Source LLC
Chambersburg PA
CBHW071720140626
46557CB00012B/986